Betsy Sikora Siino

Alaskan Malamutes

Everything about Purchase, Care, Nutrition,
Breeding, Behavior, and Training

With 47 Color Photographs

Illustrations by Tana Hakanson

BARRON'S

Photo Credits

Barbara Augello: front cover, page 9 top right; Joan Balzarini: inside back cover, page 65; Kent & Donna Dannen: pages 9 bottom, 84, 88, 92 bottom; Susan Green: pages 9 top left, 20, 28, 29 top and bottom, 32 left, 36 top, 37 top and bottom, 44 top, 57, 61, 76, 89 top and bottom; Bonnie Nance: page 72; Bob Schwartz: inside front cover, back cover, 12, 13 bottom, 16 top and bottom, 32 right, 33, 36 bottom, 40 top, 41, 44 bottom, 56, 60, 64, 77, 85, 92 top; Michael A. Siino: pages 8, 13 top, 17, 21, 45, 49, 52, 93; Judith Strom: page 40 bottom.

About the Author

Betsy Sikora Siino is an award-winning writer of books (*You Want a What For A Pet?!* and *The Siberian Husky*) and articles, primarily on subjects related to animals. As former staff writer for *Dog Fancy, Dogs USA, Pet Health News,* and *Horse Illustrated* magazines, she has a special affinity for horses, wildlife, and, most of all, for dogs, particularly for the great northern breeds (the Alaskan Malamute, the Samoyed, the American Eskimo, and the Siberian Husky among them). A graduate of the University of California at Davis, Betsy is a member of the Author's Guild and the Dog Writers Association of America (from which she was awarded Maxwell Medallions for her work on wolf/dog hybrids and wild canids). She has a special interest in subjects related to wild species and their survival, and has received acclaim for her work on wolves, coyotes and other wild predators, as well as on such controversial issues as the Endangered Species Act and the preservation of wild lands.

All inquiries should be addressed to:
Barron's Educational Series, Inc.
250 Wireless Boulevard
Hauppauge, NY 11788

International Standard Book No. 0-7641-0018-1

Library of Congress Catalog Card No. 96-44417

Library of Congress Cataloging-in-Publication Data
Siino, Betsy Sikora.
    Alaskan Malamutes : everything about purchase, care, nutrition, breeding, behavior, and training / Betsy Sikora Siino ; illustrations by Tana Hakanson.
        p.   cm.—(A complete pet owner's manual)
    Includes index.
    ISBN 0-7641-0018-1
    1. Alaskan Malamute. I. Title. II. Series.
SF429.A67S55   1997
636.73—dc21
                                            96-44417
                                            CIP

Printed in Hong Kong

987654

Important Note

This pet owner's guide tells the reader how to buy and care for an Alaskan Malamute. The author and the publisher consider it important to point out that the advice given in the book is meant primarily for normally developed puppies from a good breeder—that is, dogs of excellent physical health and good character.

Anyone who adopts a fully grown dog should be aware that the animal has already formed its basic impressions of human beings. The new owner should watch the animal carefully, including its behavior toward humans, and should meet the previous owner. If the dog comes from a shelter, it may be possible to get some information on the dog's background and peculiarities there. There are dogs that, as a result of bad experiences with humans, behave in an unnatural manner or may even bite. Only people that have experience with dogs should take in such animals.

Caution is further advised in the association of children with dogs, in meeting with other dogs, and in exercising the dog without a leash.

Even well-behaved and carefully supervised dogs sometimes do damage to someone else's property or cause accidents. It is therefore in the owner's interest to be adequately insured against such eventualities, and we strongly urge all dog owners to purchase a liability policy that covers their dog.

Contents

Preface

Northern Light—
The Alaskan Malamute

Why, some among us might wonder, would anyone be interested in a dog that may not sit when you ask it to sit, has much difficulty walking at the heel, and seems to conveniently forget all it has been taught (or to develop an unexplained temporary loss of hearing) at the most inopportune moments? Aren't dogs meant to strive for obedience, to do our every bidding, and to sit anxiously at our feet awaiting our next command? Some dogs are, perhaps, but not the Alaskan Malamute.

What this dog's critics do not realize—and despite the animal's breathtaking beauty and infectious grin, it does have its critics—is that the Malamute is always listening. It receives and understands every word we say, every subtle gesture we make. It just seems to consider itself above all that dog obedience business, viewing itself instead as equal partner with the humans in its life. It would seem it has deserved such a distinction.

For thousands of years, the Alaskan Malamute stood prominently on equal footing with humans. It learned very early in its evolution that its reason for being was to use its brains, wit and canine sixth sense to protect those odd two-legged creatures for whom it had developed quite a legendary affection. It succeeded magnificently in this mission, saving the lives of countless Arctic natives and newcomers alike, who would have met rather untimely, not to mention uncomfortable, ends in the permafrost. If con-

temporary Malamutes thus decide, on occasion, that they do not care to sit or fetch a ball, perhaps it is because they have concerns of greater import on their minds.

There is a lovely scene in the classic Disney film *The Lion King,* when young Simba learns from his father that the stars in the sky are the spirits of the kings that came before, and that they are always there to guide and protect the mortals still bound to the earth. During those inevitable moments when it appears that the Malamute, ever dignified in its demeanor, has been transported to another world, I think of that scene. I like to imagine that as the dog looks off into the distance, perhaps ignoring a *down* command, it is communing with all the Malamutes that came before, their spirits manifested not in the stars but in the northern lights. I like to believe that theirs are the voices that guide this dog across the ice and bolster its value system that to this day embodies a profound love of the human species. If I were stranded in the Arctic, I would take great comfort in knowing a Malamute, and all the Malamutes that came before, were by my side.

Acknowledgments

This book is the culmination of a lifelong love of dogs in general, and of the great northern dogs in particular. For more than 30 years, I have studied dogs voraciously; for the past 10 years I have been privileged to make writing about them my profession.

While I was able to call upon a great deal of naturally accumulated knowledge for the writing of this book, the work would not have been complete without the specialized input from some very dedicated people who were willing to share with me their own personal experiences living day-to-day with Malamutes. I extend special thanks to Roberta Steele, of Arctic-Luv Kennels in California, who, together with her dogs, showed me a great deal of hospitality and shared much valuable information, and to Virginia Devaney of the Alaskan Malamute Protection League, who works so hard, often against unspeakable odds, for the benefit of this magnificent animal.

I further appreciate the information I gathered from some of the breed's movers and shakers: AKC Malamute judge and breeder Kimberly Meredith, renowned Malamute breeder Sandy D'Andrea, and AKC Working Group judge and Malamute historian Sheila Balch. I thank them all for their time and their great knowledge.

I extend my gratitude as well to the hardworking Barron's team: Grace Freedson, for so graciously and enthusiastically recruiting me for this project, and Mary Falcon, for guiding me through a fascinating publishing experience and inviting me to participate in areas of production often kept off limits to writers.

My thanks must also go out to the Alaskan Malamute itself, a dog that has inspired me since childhood and that still makes my heart stop every time I see it, its head held high, its tail invariably wagging as though everyone it sees is its long-lost, kindred soul.

And finally, thanks to my family— Michael, Christopher, and Rebel—all of whom offered me endless moral support as I juggled the writing of this book with the responsibilities of caring for a newborn baby. This book will always be a special one to me.

—Betsy Sikora Siino

Introducing the Alaskan Malamute

An Ancient Past

We call it the last frontier, the land of the midnight sun. But to those who know and love dogs, Alaska is much more than a vast, frozen wilderness that sits at the top of the world—it is home to the magnificent Alaskan Malamute.

The true beginnings of this dog will always remain a mystery. All we are privileged to know is that the earliest ancestors of all of the great northern dog breeds lived among early representatives of our own species for thousands of years. Because of the interdependent relationship they have for so long enjoyed with our species, they were probably some of the first dogs to have been domesticated.

In light of so rich a heritage, the Malamute is believed to have bred true for centuries, if not millennia, sculpted in the biological tradition of evolution by its Arctic homeland and the people who carved out a living there.

Hailing from the Kotzebue Sound on Alaska's northwest coast, the Malamute takes its name from the native Eskimos, or Inuits, who resided there known as the Mahlemuts. Living as they did in a land of very little vegetation and frigid temperatures, these people depended on dogs for their very survival. The Mahlemuts relied on dogs not only as partners for hunting large game that was more often than not located far from home, but also, once successful in their mission, to haul that large game home over vast expanses of frozen tundra. The dogs that could fulfill this duty had to be powerful and muscular with impeccable instincts, stamina, and endurance, attributes far more critical than speed.

Blessed as they were with these quintessential freighting dogs, the Mahlemut people did not require large teams of dogs to meet the challenges of their daily lives—yet another gift Malamutes brought to their namesake humans. The Malamutes provided more muscle per dog, and their efficient metabolisms required less fuel than one would expect from so large an animal.

Alaskan Malamutes evolved as freighting dogs among the Mahlemut people of Alaska's Kotzebue Sound.

The Malamute Heart

Beyond simply taking the name of their human family, Alaska's Malamutes became veritable mirrors of the people with whom they shared their lives. The dogs and their humans evolved together, through the centuries taking on similar characteristics that enhanced the interdependence upon which their mutual survival relied.

Examples of this phenomenon existed in every aspect of the Mahlemuts' lives. Out of necessity, for example, the Mahlemut people were tireless workers. The greatest insult they could level against one of their dogs was to expect it to sit idle—or, worse yet, to leave it at home when it came time to embark on a hunt. The Mahlemuts knew that their survival required cooperation and teamwork. Their dogs, though they could be predatory and argumentative, also understood that all must work together for the survival of both the canine and human members of the team. The Mahlemuts were strong and independent, and so, of course were their dogs. Out on the ice, the people, in fact, trusted their dogs' instincts over their own, thus placing their very lives in the care of their animals.

Even on a more benign plane, the people and their dogs mirrored one another, especially where children were concerned. The Mahlemuts loved children and treated them with kindness and respect. Their dogs bonded with the young of the village, too, thus spawning a legendary love for children that remains one of the breed's most outstanding characteristics today.

From work to play to the way in which they viewed the world, the Mahlemut people could not have survived without their dogs, who not only made their peoples' daily lives possible, but no doubt brightened their days, as well.

Hailing as it does from the Arctic, an Alaskan Malamute can withstand the frigid temperatures found at the top of the world.

Dog of Legend and Lore

That the Mahlemut people treasured their dogs goes without saying. But while many treated their Malamutes almost as family members—better, in fact, than most Arctic people treated their dogs—life was harsh for humans and dogs in those Arctic settlements. Both dogs and humans had to deal with the often cruel realities of their everyday existence. When food was scarce, the dogs suffered right along with their people, and, at the mercy as they were of treacherous climate and terrain, when dogs misbehaved or failed to hold up their end of the work, they were rarely given a second chance to correct their ways.

Nevertheless, the bond that existed between the Mahlemuts and their dogs was unique, and the esteem with which the people held their canine partners was genuine. This fact did not escape the notice of the first explorers who ventured into this frozen, long unknown corner of the world in the 1800s. Upon their arrival, these adventurers invariably sang the praises of the dogs that, unlike so many other Arctic dogs, were not only partners in survival, but pets as well.

For centuries Alaskan Malamutes have shared a deep affection for, and partnership with, humans.

in 1896. As happens whenever that magical word "gold" is uttered, Alaska and the Yukon were inundated by people in search of wealth, many of them spurred on by legends of fist-sized nuggets lying on the beaches and by the romantic tales of Jack London.

London is often credited with drawing the world's attention, not only to the adventures of life in Alaska, but also to the dogs that inhabited that frozen world. While his dogs and their often vicious behavior tended to be products of the author's imagination, he vividly illuminated the bond between Alaska's dogs and their men, and the world could not help but listen.

What rang most true in London's writings was the transition that was occurring at the time of the gold rush in Alaska's canine culture. Here lived a unique collection of dogs that for centuries had been bred and raised to pull sleds across the frozen tundra, and to live their lives in symbiotic cohabitation with those few humans who were either born to life at the top of the world, or were called there in search of gold, independence, or freedom from the law.

While most prospectors sought the services of freighting dogs (a calling to which the Malamute was historically suited), and many began to fill their idle hours pitting their dogs against each other in weight-pulling contests (another natural Malamute calling), it was the racing of the dogs that drew the most enthusiastic following.

While the Malamute had handily earned the title of Alaska's premier freighting dog, the vocation of dog racing was better suited for smaller, lighter dogs that could reach and sustain greater speeds than the large Malamute was capable of. Consequently, the Malamute's bloodlines, along with others, were used for the development of what would become the favored racers: the Siberian husky and

The dogs were subsequently immortalized in the journals kept by these newcomers, who could not resist the beauty of the animals, the warmth of their personalities, and the bond they shared with their caretakers. While indeed the dogs of the frozen north, whether Malamute, Siberian husky, or Samoyed, had to be tough, with few exceptions they were also infinitely loyal to the humans in their lives. The immortality these northern dogs found in those early writings was only the beginning.

Enter the Outsiders

The trickle of explorers that came to Alaska throughout the 1800s became a flood with the discovery of gold there

The Alaskan Malamute is named for the Mahlemut people of Alaska's Kotzebue Sound. Together these people and their dogs carved out an existence in one of the world's most treacherous terrains.

A team of Alaskan Malamutes pulls a sled along a pristine, snow-covered trail.

the Alaskan husky. Because of similarities in markings, the Malamute is often mistaken for the smaller, lightweight, even delicate, Siberian. With a broader head, at least double the size, and a calmer temperament than its Siberian counterpart, the Malamute has remained a better freighter than a racer.

In the Line of Duty

As the twentieth century progressed, word of the Malamute's indomitable strength, stamina, courage, and heart reached those who were organizing Admiral Richard E. Byrd's expeditions to the South Pole. Among the dogs recruited for the two journeys to the bottom of the world were Malamutes, many of which ultimately suffered injury and illness and met cruel ends. Yet the successful exploration of this vast continent could not have been accomplished without the dogs.

The same can be said for the Malamute's contribution to America's efforts in World War II. Having already proven their mettle in Alaska and the South Pole, Malamutes were next recruited to serve as army dogs during the war.

Because of their natural talents, Malamutes were used to pull sleds in snow-covered areas that were inaccessible to other, more mechanical means of transportation. They were similarly used as pack animals to carry weaponry and ammunition across the frozen ground, and they served as search-and-rescue dogs, a task made possible by their ancient abilities to navigate endless fields of ice and snow. Again, many of the dogs perished in the line of duty, a sad fate to which the Malamute had long been accustomed.

Official Recognition

No longer shrouded in Alaska's ice and snow, after the turn of the century the reputation of the Alaskan Malamute spread south to people with more recreational goals in mind. Particularly interested in this dynamic dog were canine devotees in New England who were just beginning to embrace the new sport of sled dog racing. In the course of their discovery, several of these people found themselves enamored of the Malamute.

The breed was not in good shape at the time. The crossbreeding of Malamutes in Alaska with such breeds as Saint Bernards and similar giants, due to the lack of enough native dogs to meet the demands of the gold hunters seeking large freighting dogs, led to a severe decline in the pure Malamute population and an all-around degeneration during the gold rush of the ancient gene pool. This situation was rectified in time, however, by those fledgling breeders in the lower forty-eight who took it upon themselves to ensure that the Malamute would be preserved and remain pure for all time. Their success in this mission ultimately led to the official recognition of the Alaskan Malamute by the American Kennel Club in 1935.

The Modern Malamute

Where legends are concerned, none is more prevalent in the story of the Malamute than the belief that this dog simply must be part wolf, a legend that reached a fever pitch during the gold rush days. How else, ask those who continue to embrace this notion, could it have developed such a wolflike appearance? Yet, despite the commonly held belief that the Mahlemuts would tether a bitch to a pole in the snow so she could be bred by a wolf, countless historians, and the Mahlemut people themselves, insist the Malamute is pure domestic dog, no closer genetically than any other dog to the lupine branch of the canine family.

Get to know today's Malamute, and the obvious differences between it and the wolf are clear. While some similarities exist, such as that breathtakingly beautiful physique, a tendency to howl, and a lack of talent as a watchdog, the Malamute, unlike the wolf, has lived intimately with humans for thousands of years, evident today in the unique affection it harbors for the human species.

Today's Malamute carries on the heritage of its predecessors. It continues to revel in the family pack, to crave human companionship, and to enjoy a special affinity for children. It continues to excel as a sled dog, thriving when the thermometer's mercury drops below the freezing point, and even competing in weight-pulling competitions when the opportunity arises. And it continues to seek adventure in its daily life.

Success in a partnership with a Malamute, therefore, requires an owner who is willing to learn the Malamute's story and to respect the significance of it. The modern Malamute must be viewed in light of the ancient Malamute—the two cannot be separated. An individual willing to make this effort, one who shares the same wild and adventurous spirit of this ancient breed, is the individual with whom the Malamute will be most comfortable—and the individual who will be most content living with this magnificent animal.

Before You Make Your Decision

A Malamute in the House

The Alaskan Malamute, for obvious reasons, appeals to those attracted to the majestic countenance of the wolf. Resembling that wild creature as closely as it does, the Malamute brings the ancient spirit of the North into the daily lives of mere mortals who don't happen to reside in the last frontier.

The popular media has enthusiastically embraced the Malamute's wolflike image, casting Malamutes as body doubles for their wild cousins. This, however, often results in a negative public response not only to the "vicious" man-eating wolf the Malamute is asked to impersonate, but also to the Malamute itself, which is then mistaken by those ignorant of such matters as a vicious wolflike dog on city streets. This has occurred repeatedly in preposterous scenes in movies and television shows, in which packs of smiling Malamutes, their lush, curled tails wagging in unison, "threaten" to devour lost hikers or various and sundry action heroes.

Though such media imagery has caused some to fear the Malamute, others can think of no finer pet than this beautiful, rather challenging beast with the look of the wolf and the ancient soul of the Arctic.

Given the Malamute's rich and rather arduous past, it is remarkable that the breed has remained pure. Although it is probably larger today, the Malamute probably still resembles very closely the original Malamutes of the Arctic. Then as now, the Malamute continues to grace the homes in which it resides with the gifts it has acquired through thousands of years of living with humans, attributes that can be traced to a life as companion, lifeline, and soulmate. Only those who appreciate this heritage should dare to invite this unique animal into their homes.

Are You the Right Owner for a Malamute?

Malamutes demand much from their owners. They demand to occupy prominent positions in their family packs; they demand to play central roles in every family activity; and they demand that their instincts, body language, and

The noble wolflike countenance of the Alaskan Malamute tends to be the first characteristic that draws people to this breed.

vocalizations be respected and, when appropriate, heeded. In exchange, they willingly return tenfold to the worthy owner what is given to them.

Yet that owner cannot be a run-of-the-mill individual. This individual, like the Malamute itself, must possess an adventurous, yet sensitive heart. This does not mean he or she must take daily forays out on to the glacier, but each day must be ripe with some sort of activity in which the dog, too, can participate.

Also critical to the relationship is the understanding that Malamutes possess an acute sensitivity to all the goings-on in their households and to the dynamics between family members. They react instinctively to the most subtle body positions and vocal inflections, especially during arguments and moments of strife, and they expect their owners to be just as sensitive toward them.

Learning Canine Language

In return, the owner should learn all he or she can, from books, trainers, behaviorists, and from experience with the dog itself, about canine language. One of the greatest insults to the Malamute is an owner who does not try to communicate succinctly with his or her dog. For thousands of years this animal has lived among people who offered it that respect inherent to their mutual communication. To do otherwise could mean death to both the people and the dogs, when, say, the musher guiding the sled failed to heed the lead dog's warning of a crevasse in the ice or some other pending danger of which the dog's sixth sense warned.

This type of relationship is what the Malamute continues to expect from those humans it calls family. As the relationship blossoms, owners begin to take for granted the fact that the dog seems practically able to read their minds, to respond to their human thoughts even before they have dared to acknowledge them themselves.

The deep loyalty exhibited by the Alaskan Malamute to the human species has been known to bring tears to the eyes of those privileged to live with this dog.

While far gentler in character than one might expect for so large a dog, the Alaskan Malamute can become a dominant, overbearing animal if it is allowed to go through life undisciplined.

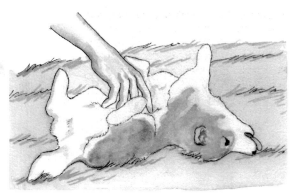

While a young Malamute puppy may be irresistible, it will someday grow into a very large dog in need of an owner dedicated to discipline and consistency.

Given its history, it should come as no surprise that the Malamute is considered one of the canine family's most people-loving members. And it rarely discriminates in this mission. Although its size, as well as its wolflike appearance, will surely keep disreputable types at bay, owners learn quickly that these dogs will gladly welcome strangers into their homes and probably lead them right to the valuables while they're at it!

Who's the Boss?

Malamute owners also learn very quickly that the breed is one of the strongest willed and most independent members of the canine family tree. Without these attributes, the dogs would have perished on the ice, never surviving to see the twentieth century. But they did survive, as did their independent natures. As a result, they require owners who are more than just patient, but accepting, as well. Nevertheless, it is critical from the very beginning that the dog learn that it is not the boss.

This does not mean it should be beaten into submission or otherwise mistreated. Rather, the best way to convince this pack-sensitive dog that it is subordinate is through such subtle tactics as assigning it a spot other than your bed as its sleeping place and insisting, with firmness and consistency, that it obey your commands every time without fail. It need not perform the perfect *sit* or *heel,* but it must understand that you mean business. You can help get this message across to the dog most effectively during its puppyhood, when you must resist the desire to overindulge the adorable youngster. Spoil the pup, and you will end up with a demanding, potentially aggressive 100-pound (45.4 kg) dog that is suddenly deaf in both ears whenever you issue a command.

The Malamute's independent nature is often mistaken for a lack of intelligence, often by trainers who are more accustomed to working with the likes of willing Golden Retrievers. While "stubborn" may be a valid label for this dog, veteran Malamute keepers would never accuse their breed of a lack of intelligence. You simply have to make its lessons interesting, that's all. The trick is to convince the dog that there is a good reason for it to do what you are asking it to do. Never underestimate this animal's understanding of what you are teaching it. Assuming you are clear and consistent with your instructions, it's a safe bet the dog will understand quickly. Whether or not it will deign to obey, however, is another story, as it may choose instead to test the intensity of your resolve.

Keeping Your Malamute Busy

Boredom and Malamutes don't mix. This dog is generally happiest learning more complex, purposeful skills, say, those required to pull a sled through a blizzard or to accompany an owner on cross-country skis. In other words, this dog must be kept busy, both physically and mentally, or those abundant energies may just have to be vented in more destructive directions—perhaps in tearing apart the living room furniture or digging trenches in the backyard. A dog of this size and strength can do quite a lot of damage when it sets its mind to it.

An Owner's Resumé

Put yourself in the Malamute's place. Given its ancestral heritage, how do you measure up to the individual it would choose as, if it could choose, its owner? Living with a Malamute is dramatically different from living with most other breeds of dog, so before you take that plunge and decide to buy a Malamute, evaluate your Malamute-ownership resumé from the dog's point of view:

Where do you live? Yes, the ideal domicile for a Malamute is a house with a large yard, but this is not to say that the dog must be simply banished to life outdoors never to set foot in the house. Inherent in this breed's love of people is the need to share its people's lives fully. Malamutes do enjoy and require ample time outdoors, but they also relish the opportunity to spend the evening by the fire in the company of family. The Malamute can reside in a more cramped dwelling, even one without large acreage surrounding it, but only if it is offered a great deal of exercise and mental stimulation every single day—a requirement true of any Malamute in any living situation.

What is your dog experience? If they had their "druthers," Malamute rescuers and reputable breeders would prefer that only those with experience with dogs—especially experience with large, headstrong dogs—take the step into the adventure that is the Alaskan Malamute. Newcomers can succeed, but they must be willing to do their homework and find mentors who can help them along.

What are your expectations? Before you even begin contemplating the prospect of living with a Malamute, you must honestly evaluate the reality of living with a savvy, strong-willed dog that can ultimately weigh as much as 100, 110, even 120 pounds (45.4, 49.9, 54 kg). Do you have the time, inclination, and physical and temperamental ability required to mold the behavior of so complex, even dominant, an animal in positive directions? Do you truly want a dog that demands to be an integral part of every project, every activity? Are you active enough for a partnership with a Malamute? This isn't an exercise machine you purchase with grand resolutions to "get in shape," only to cast it away in a corner once the novelty and your commitment wane.

Pay attention to more practical concerns, as well:
• Will a full-grown Malamute fit in your car?
• Are there other pets in the household that may inspire predatory impulses in this dog?
• Do you mind having hair all over the furniture, in the carpet, on your clothes and in your food? If so, perhaps a Nordic dog of any breed is not appropriate for your household.

What about the rest of the family? If there are children about, that will certainly please the resident Malamute, but the kids and dog must be monitored to prevent any unforeseen mishaps that can occur between a young child and a very large dog. As for the young Malamute, everyone must be warned that it will not remain the roly-poly teddy-bear-like puppy for long. Are all in the family willing to commit to this soon-to-be-large and potentially domineering dog's training and socialization, to practice consistency, and to refuse to allow the pup to engage in behaviors that will be forbidden once the dog is grown?

Can you afford a Malamute? The proper care of any dog can be costly, what with veterinary care, kenneling,

Most Malamutes sport a cap and/or a mask of color on their faces and heads.

equipment, food, etc., but a Malamute, for obvious reasons, is particularly costly to feed, house, board, and transport.

Another expense associated with Malamute keeping is that of the time involved. In addition to the time required for daily exercise and activity, you may need to divide your dog's daily food rations into two or three small meals a day to keep the dog more comfortable and to prevent the deadly condition of canine bloat (see page 68). Also time consuming can be the grooming of this dog, which requires regular and very thorough brushing, especially when the coat is shedding.

Can you offer a lifetime commitment? You don't have to be born with a natural sensitivity to and understanding of the nuances of Malamute communication, but the successful human partner of this dog will exhibit a genuine desire to master these skills. You must commit not only to the dog, but to your own patience and sensitivity. Work with a trainer who understands the unique Malamute character, and who respects the breed's intelligence and the fascinating ways in which its mind works.

In reviewing your qualifications as a prospective Malamute owner, ask yourself and your family the proper questions and be honest with the answers. Assure yourself and your family that your desire for this breed runs far deeper than simply wishing for a beautiful dog that many will mistake for a wolf. Success is greatest for those who feel a true kinship with this animal and see that as their motivation for living with one.

After all of this soul searching, should you determine that you are genuinely motivated to forge the strong bond that can exist between Malamutes and their people, you have a big job ahead of you.

The Ideal Malamute

Next on the agenda is to become familiar with the American Kennel Club breed standard for the Malamute, a tool that will come in handy as you begin your search for a new Malamute family member. Armed with this information, you will be prepared to evaluate the potential candidates and make the best choice possible.

Daily walks are a must if you are to raise a healthy, well-adjusted Alaskan Malamute.

The standard exists as a model for breeders, offering them an ideal to strive for in their breeding programs. The overriding goal is to keep the breed pure and breeding true. While every AKC breed has a standard, the Malamute, as a member of the AKC Working Group, is bred according to a standard in which form follows function. Bred to work, Malamutes are judged in the show ring for their potential as working sledge dogs, and their conformation must lend itself to that purpose.

General Appearance

The Malamute should present a strong, dignified, powerful picture of a dog with a deep chest, a straight back, and a lushly furred curled tail that the dog carries proudly over its back.

Engineered for pulling sleds and sledges over treacherous terrain, the Malamute's legs should be large boned and well muscled, coupled with equally large feet with thick pads insulated by a dense growth of hair. Atop its wide, thickly muzzled head, its erect, wedge-shaped ears remain alert to the most subtle of sounds. The dog's noble, often serenely intelligent gaze emanates from its almond-shaped eyes, which should be brown (blue eyes, acceptable in Siberian huskies, are a disqualifying fault in Malamutes).

Size

While Malamutes are found in a range of sizes, the average male, as reflected in the standard, stands about 25 inches (63.5 cm) at the shoulder and weighs in at approximately 85 pounds (38.6 kg); the female is slightly smaller, standing approximately 23 inches (58 cm) at the shoulder and weighing in at 75 pounds (34 kg). Many Malamutes are much larger than this, however, and, assuming they are physically proportioned and sport the correct movement and structure, the larger dogs are rarely penalized in the

While black and shades of gray are the traditional Malamute colors, a rare red variation with lighter eyes is also acceptable.

show ring. There is danger, however, in modern trends that encourage the breeding of giant Malamutes—dogs that can reach as much as 150 pounds (68 kg). Such excess size and weight can stress the dog's muscles and bones, and theories suggest that they may stress the heart, as well.

Color

The typical Malamute is usually gray in color, ranging from a very light gray to black, with white undersides, although pure white and a rare red variation with lighter eyes is also acceptable. The dog's coat color is usually complemented by either a mask of color across the dog's white face or a cap of color at the top of its head, markings that, despite all-around similarities in color, differentiate it clearly from a wolf.

Coat

Like all members of the Nordic family of dogs, the Malamute sports a thick double coat, consisting of a soft, woolly

Because puppies require a great deal of time and effort to raise properly, an adult Malamute may be a more appropriate pet for some families.

undercoat that acts as an insulator, combined with a longer, rather coarse coat of guard hairs that stand out from the dog's body. This ingenious system protects the dog in those legendary sub-zero temperatures of its homeland, yet with ample shade and constant access to fresh cool water, today's pet Malamute should fare well in warmer climes, as well. When temperatures are extreme, such as 100°F (37.8°C) and above, the dog should be kept indoors during the day and exercised only when the heat subsides. The owner should also resist the temptation to shave the coat. Veteran owners cringe at the thought, knowing that Malamutes do not adjust well emotionally to the removal of one of its primary physical characteristics.

Temperament
The standard addresses the Malamute's temperament, as well. In keeping with the dog's ancient past, today's Malamute is described in its breed standard as loyal, affectionate, friendly, dignified, and devoted. With this standard guiding its breeding, it is little wonder that the well-bred Malamute commands such enthusiasm from its human companions.

Adult or Puppy?
Once you have come to understand the mechanics of evaluating Malamutes

effectively, you must decide just what kind of Malamute you want—an adult or a puppy.

Each has its benefits and each has its drawbacks. While many people dream of bringing a new puppy into the house and raising it into the lovely adult it is destined to be, doing this right requires a great deal of time and effort.

To raise a puppy correctly, you must, for all practical purposes, become the young dog's surrogate mom and commit to molding it into a well-behaved adult. This, as any mom can testify, can be a full-time job. Obedience training, household manners, housetraining, and socialization are the ingredients that lead to a well-behaved adult Malamute. Such a dog does not occur as a natural phenomenon; it is the product of hours of nurturing, sweat, and consistency.

Those who honestly do not believe they have the time to raise a puppy, but believe they must have a Malamute in the house, may be more interested in adopting an older dog that has already received its basic education and experienced the challenging trials of puppy adolescence. In fact, many have found they prefer a dog that is five or six years of age, as this dog will tend to be more settled, its youthful exuberance will have mellowed somewhat, and it will be more content devoting its time to its duties as family companion. If you overcome the prejudice too many people harbor against bringing an older dog into the home, you may just find a treasure.

Launching the Treasure Hunt
Once upon a time, Alaskan Malamutes could be found only in Alaska. Today, fortunately for those who seek to live with one of these dogs, you may find fine specimens without making a pilgrimage to the land of the midnight sun.

The Breeder
Should you decide that you would like to purchase an Alaskan Malamute

from a breeder, which many consider the ideal source for a purebred puppy, you will need to be prepared not only to choose the right puppy or dog, but also the right breeder. The best way to do this is to contact several, and find out how they operate.

In the purest sense, the reputable, ethical breeder breeds not for profit, but out of a true devotion to a breed. Such breeders are well aware of the genetic problems inherent in their breed and do all they can to prevent them in their lines. They take a great deal of care in placing their puppies in good homes, interviewing buyers extensively and turning down anyone who doesn't seem up to their standards. Their dogs can be expensive, but in most cases, you are getting what you pay for.

The best breeders will guarantee their dogs against genetic problems, will offer a full refund if such problems arise, and will agree in writing to take their dogs back in the future at any time, for any reason. In working with such a breeder, you may find a variety of dogs available. You may place your name on a waiting list for a young puppy, or decide that a retired show or sled Malamute is more appropriate for your lifestyle. The key is to be patient. An impulse buy will reduce the odds of your forging the lifelong bond that every Malamute—every dog—deserves.

What too many potential buyers mistakenly believe is that breeders produce only show dogs. If fact, most puppies in a particular litter will be of pet quality. Given the value of a precious family pet, this simply means that the pet-quality puppy deviates in often subtle ways from the breed standard, but borne of the same bloodlines and diligence that begets the show champion, that pet-quality pup radiates with the same health and vitality.

When meeting with a breeder of such animals, evaluate the overall breeding operation:

- Is the facility clean?
- Do the dogs look healthy, friendly, and well cared for?
- Is the breeder knowledgeable about both the breed and his or her dogs?
- Does the breeder seem committed more to the dogs or to potential profits?
- Does the breeder guarantee his or her stock?

The ethical breeder will question the prospective buyer just as extensively as the buyer questions the breeder to ensure that the puppies will find a proper and permanent home. This breeder will also conduct the sale via contract (a breeder without a contract should be avoided), and a commitment to the Malamute Club's Code of Ethics will be reflected in that contract.

The Contract: Such a contract is beneficial to all parties involved: buyer, breeder, and dog. It protects the new owner by guaranteeing the genetic health of the dog and its parents; it demands contractually that pet animals be spayed or neutered (a provision backed up by the AKC's Limited Registration, which will not issue regular registration papers to a dog officially designated as a pet by its breeder); and it will allow the owner to return the dog if he or she can no longer keep it in the future. Such guarantees, combined with healthy, well-bred Malamutes from which to choose, add up to a successful breeder/buyer transaction, and a long-term Malamute/owner relationship.

The Animal Shelter

What many prospective dog owners do not realize is that the nation's animal shelters are filled not only with mixed-breed dogs, but with purebreds as well. Even the friendly, majestic Malamute is often found awaiting a new home from behind the chain link of an animal shelter, typically the victim of an owner who was ill-prepared to care for and work with such a dog.

Work only with a breeder who sells his or her dogs with a detailed contract that guarantees the animal's health and soundness, and who agrees to take the dog back should you be unable to keep it in the future.

Puppies should be introduced to a variety of new sights, sounds, and people throughout their formative years to help them to grow into stable, well-adjusted adults.

If you find a Malamute in a shelter, it will most likely be an older adolescent puppy or a mature adult, cast aside by people who adored the dog when it was a puppy that resembled a young wolf, but whose interest waned when confronting the monumental commitment of caring for the full-grown Malamute. Do not let this situation discourage you. With the proper commitment from its owner, this dog, too, can become a fine pet.

The adopted shelter Malamute will probably be in need of some rehabilitation, best pursued with the help of a canine behaviorist well versed in both Malamute character and in the special needs of the adopted shelter dog. While this Malamute may be headstrong and lacking in the early socialization that is best conducted during puppyhood, its people-loving nature will help it to fit readily into the family, inspiring all to face the challenge of adjustment and training with enthusiasm.

The Breed Rescue Organization

Within some breeds there exists a network of breeders who devote their time not only to producing fine examples of the breed, but also to rescuing those dogs that have fallen through the cracks and become lost, abandoned, or otherwise victimized by inappropriate owners. The Malamute is one of those.

While there will always be Malamutes that fail to be rescued, the Alaskan Malamute Protection League, Inc., a national network that works with Malamute rescue groups across the nation, tracks available dogs and sets standard policies on how they should be fostered and adopted. While the League cannot save them all, its goal is to keep the number of homeless, unwanted Malamutes to a minimum. Rescue is carried out by volunteers who take the dogs in from private owners and shelters, and then match them up with new owners who will offer them a second chance at the life and commitment they deserve.

As with shelter dogs, rescue dogs are typically older. In working with a good rescue group, prospective owners, who are carefully screened for their fitness for life with a Malamute, can often feel confident in their choice of a new pet because rescue dogs are generally kept in foster homes. In such an environment, rescue volunteers can get to know the dogs' quirks, and work to correct problems, thus easing the dogs' transitions into their new homes.

Selecting a Healthy Malamute Pet

The most valuable tool available to the potential Malamute buyer is the Code of Ethics issued by the Alaskan Malamute Club of America, the breed's national club. While there are no guarantees, a dog bred according to the tenets of the code has every chance of being the pet you dream of.

Within the code are stipulations that forbid breeders from selling puppies to entities for the breeding of wolf/dog hybrids (see discussion on wolf/dog hybrids, page 76). It addresses the genetic problems that affect Malamutes, emphasizes the need for spay/neuter contracts for non-show dogs, and states that breeders will be responsible for the dogs they produce for the lifetime of those dogs. The code, therefore, offers potential buyers a context for evaluating potential pets, as this is a choice that must be made with the mind rather than the heart.

For this critical evaluation process, several factors come into play. Male Malamutes, for example, tend to be larger and more domineering than their female counterparts, and puppies may be more difficult to evaluate objectively because of the "cuteness" factor. While the significance of such elements will vary depending on whether you are buying a show puppy or adopting a rescue dog, it is best to be as informed as possible about the breed and thus about the dogs you will be meeting.

Meeting Mom and Dad

If it's a puppy you are seeking, you can pick up some important clues as to what your prospective pet will be like when it matures by meeting the youngster's parents. Temperament, health, and conformation can all be passed on from one generation to the next, so meeting Mom and Dad can help you evaluate certain characteristics inherent in a particular Malamute family.

Meeting Mom is especially critical, because the quality of her maternal instincts can have long-term effects on how the puppy interacts with people and other dogs. Steer clear of puppies from a shy, timid, and/or aggressive dam, as her behavior may be passed on both genetically and by example to her offspring, even if she is with them for only the first eight weeks of life.

While it may prove a difficult task, choosing a healthy, well-adjusted Malamute puppy must be done with the head as well as the heart.

Note: Be suspicious of the breeder who is willing to allow a puppy to leave its mom before it reaches seven weeks of age.

A friendly, nurturing mom, on the other hand, who is attentive to her young family and affectionate toward the humans in her life, will offer even very young puppies a positive role model whose early care will leave an indelible imprint on her puppies' adult behavior.

The Genetic Blueprint

The Alaskan Malamute, like virtually every breed of dog, is prone to several genetic conditions, including hip dysplasia, night blindness, chondrodysplasia (dwarfism that results in deformed limbs), and hypothyroidism. The incidence of these can be reduced by breeders who, in heeding the Malamute Club's Code of Ethics, refrain from breeding affected dogs, and by educated puppy buyers who purchase puppies only from parents that are unaffected by these conditions.

The key word here is "educated." The well-informed buyer will choose puppies whose parents have been certified as free of hip dysplasia by the Orthopedic Foundation for Animals (the OFA has recently begun tracking hypothyroidism as well), and of chondrodysplasia by the national breed club. The breeder should further guarantee in the purchase contract that his or her stock is free of the breed's genetic anomalies. The ethical breeder will be impressed by a buyer's knowledge of these potential problems. If the breeder is insulted by your inquiries, look elsewhere.

Health and Temperament

Whether you are seeking a puppy or an adult Malamute, a sound evaluation of your prospective pet relies on your own knowledge of the breed standard, general canine health, and canine temperament. While you may be tempted to purchase or adopt a dog from the first breeder, shelter, or rescue foster home you visit, meeting as many dogs as possible will help you make a more informed choice.

On the health front, look for a dog with clear eyes and a lustrous, uniformly healthy coat, both of which can be effective indicators of internal health and the quality of the dog's diet and breeding. Despite the accepted myth, the dog's nose need not be cool and moist, but the animal should breathe clearly, and its ears should be clean and odor free. Armed with the breed standard, look for a Malamute that closely resembles that ideal, but don't turn the dog down if it doesn't meet or exceed that ideal—no dog does.

Temperament can be trickier, but go with your instincts. When evaluating a litter of puppies, suppress the inclination to "rescue" the shy, timid runt in the corner. Remember, you are looking for a new family member who should remain a beloved member of the clan for more than a decade to come. A better prospect is the puppy that is friendly and affectionate, outgoing and playful.

Temperament testing can be helpful to a point. Roll the animal over on its back. If it enjoys the position and remains still, it is of a more submissive nature—or may simply be tired at the moment. If it struggles desperately to right itself, it is of a more dominant head and will probably need a stronger, firmer hand to help it understand who is boss. Either one can make a fine pet, but evaluate your own abilities to work with such dogs and make your choice accordingly.

Similar considerations of health and temperament should guide your choice of an older dog, although you may not have the opportunity to visit with the dog's parents, and rolling an unknown 100-pound (45.4 kg) rescue dog over on its back can be extremely dangerous. A rescue or shelter dog, or even a retired show dog, may have a few negative habits to overcome, issues that, ideally, you can discuss with the dog's caretaker to determine whether you are up to the job of rehabilitating such an animal. Indeed, most older dogs have a wart or two, but some are more challenging than others; for example, a three-year-old that is still not housebroken may require a more experienced owner than will a five-year-old that pulls on the leash. More difficult still is the dog that has been mistreated in its past, leaving it with emotional scars that will require time and patience as well as know-how to overcome.

Finally, some dogs just plain like certain people more than others and vice versa. You may find when evaluating a litter of puppies or meeting a couple of rescue dogs, that for some unexplainable reason, you find yourself instantly drawn to one and the feelings are mutual. As with human attractions, there is no accounting for what sometimes draws us to our prospective pets. Assuming that all the other elements of level-headed evaluation are in order, heed that intuition. You may just be rewarded with a truly legendary companion for whom you become a legend, as well.

Bringing Your Malamute Home

The Puppy Layette

The waiting is almost over. Perhaps you have waited patiently for your new puppy to reach the age at which it can leave its mother, or, after several meetings, you have chosen a rescue Malamute that seems perfectly suited to your family. To ease the anticipation, take a trip to the pet supply store and stock up on what you'll need before your new pet crosses the threshold.

When deciding what supplies you will need to welcome your Malamute, determine first what type of food you will be feeding your new pet. To prevent digestive upset, it is best for the first few days to feed the dog whatever it was being fed before. Then, if you wish to switch to a different food later, do so gradually by mixing the old with the new over several days.

Rounding out the supplies are the standard items:

• food and water dishes
• safe and sturdy chew toys (fleece toys, rope bones, and Nylabones tend to be favorites)
• a brush and rake for the coat
• a leash and collar
• dog treats

Don't forget your dog's bed, which will require such items as a crate, blankets, towels, pillows, an exercise pen—whatever you have deemed necessary for your new pet's home within your home. Such preparation will make the adjustment smoother and easier for everyone.

Another very positive gesture is to order identification tags for your dog immediately. You may order these through most pet supply stores and veterinary offices, so start the process now and get the tag on the dog as soon as you can. Should your new pet become lost, an identification tag will be its ticket home.

The Security of Confinement

Bring your new pet home at the start of a quiet weekend, when it will be just family and dog getting acquainted. Try and view the situation through the eyes of the dog—a puppy away from its mom and its littermates for the first time, or a rescue dog mourning the separation from its foster family. Obviously, the dog will experience some sort of anxiety, which will logically translate into certain behaviors the owner deems unacceptable.

While you do not want to reward such behaviors as whimpering, barking, howling, and furniture chewing, you must be sensitive to what the dog is experiencing. Be gentle yet firm—placing a ticking clock outside of your puppy's bed to mimic its mom's heartbeat, for example, or placing your pup's bed near your bed so it can hear you breathing through the night.

All dogs should wear a properly fitting collar and current identification tag at all times.

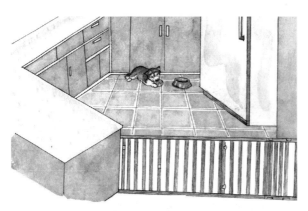

A puppy appreciates the security of an enclosed corner when you are not at home.

The Crate

The most important tool for easing your dog's adjustment into its new home is the concept of confinement, an idea you should begin to introduce from the very first night. Many do this with the help of a crate. Though crates are made for safe airline and car travel, they can work wonders in the day-to-day management of the family pet, as well.

While you may cringe at the thought of locking a puppy up in a "box," most dogs actually find their crates—well furnished with warm blankets, padding, and toys—very comforting, assuming the owner does not abuse the crate's use by insisting the dog spend the majority of its time inside it. The crate offers a denlike home to the dog, which may be convinced to try it out with a few treat motivators. Once inside, the dog discovers this isn't so bad after all. You may marvel at how peacefully a new eight-week-old puppy slumbers on that first night away from its family, ensconced in a cozy den carpeted with soft warm blankets.

Other Confinement Areas

Yet a puppy or dog can enjoy this security without a crate, as well. Try confining the dog into a specific part of the house at night and whenever you are not at home—perhaps with a roomy exercise pen set up in the kitchen or a corner of your bedroom. This will not only protect the house from a Malamute with an urge to chew furniture legs or tear up carpet on a lonely afternoon, but will also offer the dog its own little corner of the world where it can relax and revel in safety. You may be inspired to adhere to this concept by the fact that a Malamute, particularly a bored Malamute in need of exercise, could decide on a whim to use its almost supercanine strength to tear through the drywall just for fun (which it could do in a confined space, as well; hence the need for the exercise pen, which provides a barrier between dog and household walls). Punishment for such an act would be unjust, especially if you don't catch the dog in the act. This is something the right owner is prepared for and takes steps to try and prevent.

Safety

Confinement can also save a puppy's life, keeping it out of trouble when there is no one to watch out for its safety. When the youngster is allowed to roam, you should ensure that the house has been properly puppyproofed. Make sure electrical cords are hidden, and keep dangerous items, such as poisonous plants and glass Christmas tree ornaments out of the puppy's path. For much of its first year, the young puppy will be teething and need desperately to chew. Your job is to ensure that everything it finds to chew on is not only acceptable, but safe, too.

In designing your dog's safe haven, use exercise pens or similar modular enclosures, all available at large pet supply stores or through mail order, that will keep the dog confined while still allowing it to walk around and stretch. While Malamutes relish the opportunity to be indoors if that is where the family is, arrange similar accommodations outdoors as well (you cannot allow the dog to run loose in the neighborhood). Just make sure the fencing material in a fenced yard or kennel run is of the highest quality (Malamutes have been known to chew through chain link), is at least six feet (1.83 m) high, and is buried deep enough into the ground to withstand digging. If your pet is an exceptional jumper, outfit the run with a top, too.

Establishing the Routine

Just as the routine is key to housebreaking, so is it vital to helping the dog become accustomed to its new home. Even at a very young age, dogs are creatures of habit. They learn quickly to tell time, amazing their owners with their ability to figure out that mealtime is a half hour late, or their tendency to hold a vigil at the front door when it's time for the evening run.

The most effective way to ease a new dog into the household is to begin immediately to introduce it to the family patterns so it will learn its place, its role. This offers the dog a sense of security as it learns what to expect of you and what you expect of it, and it imparts the subtle message that you are the boss. One of the greatest mistakes new owners make is overindulging the dog upon its arrival, thus convincing this extremely pack-sensitive breed that it is welcome to take on the leadership role.

To establish the routine, determine how and when you will be caring for the dog, and carry out those various duties at the same times every day. Remain true, too, to scheduled daily exercise, and do the same with daily training sessions.

Maintain the element of freshness by involving the dog in other, typically non-routine activities, as well. Do you have any household repair jobs to tend to? Let your Malamute join in.

Sure, the dog's assistance may cause the job to last twice as long, but the joy the animal exhibits as it takes part in the action is worth that extra time. Is it laundry day? Well, enlist the Malamute to follow you as you carry the clothes to the laundry and encourage the dog to pick up dropped socks and other items. Are the kids hankering to play in the snow? Well, by all means send the family Malamute out to join them. Such a mix of routine and surprise can result in a Malamute that is well adjusted, content, and secure in the knowledge that its needs will be addressed diligently.

An Indoor/Outdoor Dog

The Alaskan Malamute was bred and raised as a working dog—an Arctic working dog at that. But this does not automatically mean it must be relegated exclusively to the outdoors, never to cross the threshold of the family home. Exile of this type, especially without companionship from another dog (preferably a large dog of the opposite gender) will result in a howling, destructive, and all-around miserable dog. This dog simply must share home and hearth, both indoors and out, with its human family.

Yes, this is a big dog. Yes, this is a thick-coated dog. But these are characteristics owners must ponder before choosing to live with this dog who relies on human companionship in all environments, indoors and out. While a young puppy should spend its formative months as an essentially indoor dog, as it grows, it will want to spend more and more time outdoors. As an adult, it will thrive best with balance. The fortunate Malamute is the dog that is offered indoor/outdoor accommodations: regular, though controlled, access to the house and all the wonderful activities that occur there, and to a roomy enclosure in the yard, as well.

HOW-TO:
Housebreaking Made Easy

Many a new dog owner shudders at the thought of teaching a new pet where it can eliminate and where it can't, envisioning an endless battle of wills that can severely undermine the relationship between dog and owner. Indeed, when puppy owners discuss the challenges presented by their new charges, the subject of housebreaking invariably dominates the interchange. Yet there is absolutely no need for such lamentations. Dogs truly want to learn the household rules of elimination, but they can only do so with an owner who is consistent and knowledgeable in how to impart the information in a way that dogs can understand.

The following are the basic tenets of successful housebreaking. Follow them with consistency and patience, and you will soon be proud to proclaim that your dog has been housebroken.

Implement a routine: Where housebreaking is concerned, the routine is the key to success. Puppies must eat several times a day, and thus usually must eliminate on schedule, as well. Feed your pet at the same times every day. Then, after mealtime, take the youngster outside to a particular corner of the yard where you want it to do its business (you may also choose a newspaper-covered corner of the house, but this will prove to be impractical as the pup grows, so why confuse it now?).

Now give the pup the command *"Go Potty,"* or whatever command you will be comfortable using in the years to come.

Yes, dogs can be taught to go on command, and it's never too early to begin the lessons. As soon as the puppy eliminates, praise it profusely so there is no doubt in its mind that it has done a wonderful thing.

Accentuate the positive: Your mission in this grand endeavor is to make housebreaking a positive experience for yourself and for your dog. Punishment has no place here. Positive reinforcement is everything. Praise the dog when it performs properly, and ignore any impulses to punish the animal when it doesn't. When an accident does occur, keep in mind that the mistake was probably yours. Perhaps the dog didn't understand your expectations, perhaps you missed its signals, perhaps its small bladder had been taxed to its limit, or perhaps the dog could not reach the spot where it knows you wish it to eliminate.

The dog will succeed if given the chance. After meals and whenever you return home from an absence, take the pup immediately to its proper elimination location, give the command, and praise the dog for complying. Watch the dog carefully when it is free to roam the house so you can detect the tell-tale sniffing and crouching that signal nature's call. Be patient and remain consistent in this pattern, and you will find that your puppy, or even your previously untrained adult dog, has been transformed into a gloriously housebroken dog.

Confine the pup: Just as confinement is critical to the safety of a dog, so does it come in equally handy in the chal-

After meals and naps, take the puppy outdoors to relieve itself. Encourage the pup with a command, and praise it profusely for performing.

A dog crate can be a valuable tool for housebreaking a puppy, but its use can be abused if one leaves a puppy inside for hours and hours at a time.

lenge that can be housebreaking. In your efforts to make this a positive experience for the dog, keep it confined to a specific area (preferably its designated corner of the house) when you are not home to watch its every move. You therefore create more opportunities for praise and less for mistakes.

Dealing with the inevitable: Accidents will happen, of course, but you can turn these accidents into lesson opportunities. Ignore the advice to rub the dog's nose in a calling card it has accidentally left in the house. This will only confuse the poor animal and impede your progress, especially if you punish the dog after it has had its accident (it may seem contrite in its behavior, but that is a reaction to *your* behavior, not to what it did hours or even minutes before).

If you do happen to catch the dog in the act of eliminating in the house, react immediately. Make a loud noise to startle the animal and usher it immediately to the proper location where it may finish the job. Again, praise it enthusiastically, and you will have effectively gotten your point across.

When your dog does have an accident, clean it up quickly.

While feces are easily removed, urine can soak into carpeting and similar surfaces and leave a powerful odor that owners find offensive and that invites dogs back again in the future. Use plain soap and water to clean the site of a urine accident or one of the enzymatic cleaners specifically formulated to remove, not mask, the substance. Avoid strong chemical cleaners, especially those that contain ammonia, as these will only intensify the odor.

A puppy's body language may suggest it is ashamed after having an accident, but the youngster is in fact reacting to your irritation, not to the fact that it left an illegal puddle behind hours, or even minutes, before.

Though they play hard throughout the day, puppies must be allowed to balance play sessions with a great deal of sleep and rest.

New Experiences

A new Malamute in the family has the grand responsibility of getting to know the intimate world within its family pack, as well as the world beyond its front door. Just imagine all it must learn. Assist the dog in this mission, and you will help foster the development of a wonderfully well-adjusted pet who is prepared to accompany you wherever you go.

New Places, New Faces

One word you are likely to hear whenever puppies are discussed is "socialization." Although the Alaskan Malamute is a naturally affectionate dog, because it is prone to dominant, even aggressive behavior in adulthood if overindulged as a puppy, it benefits from intensive socialization efforts that should be started as early as possible.

This can be an immensely enjoyable process, in which you expose the puppy to new experiences, places, and people—all with a very positive flair. Reward the youngster for its positive response to such new explorations, yet remain firm and consistent in handling the puppy both at home and away. Take the puppy with you wherever you go (if possible), and allow everyone to pet and play with it so it might learn just how satisfying life can be. Of course the pup must also learn to be alone to prevent it from suffering in the future from separation anxiety, which can manifest itself in barking, chewing, and all-around destruction.

Because Malamutes don't always get along with others of their own kind (especially males with males and females with females), introduce the pup to other dogs, as well. Larger dogs are usually preferable to smaller dogs in this endeavor, as smaller dogs may be seen as prey to the predatory Malamute. Allow the pup to play and wrestle and learn just how delightful others of its own kind can be. Invite friends and family to your house frequently, so the puppy will also grow accustomed to human visitors—a rather simple stretch for this dog that

Malamutes love being part of every family activity. Take advantage of this fact and enlist the dog to help out with household chores.

is known more for showing strangers where the valuables are stored than in protecting family heirlooms.

Newcomers to the Malamute breed may mistake this breed's affinity for humans and its somewhat laughable skills as a guard dog with a complete lack of dominance or aggression. Beware: Such a mistake can spell danger. Any dog can be aggressive, including the people-loving Malamute, so remember the advice offered by Virginia Devaney of the Alaskan Malamute Protection League: Never leave a Malamute alone with a young child, and never leave a Malamute alone with others of its own kind. While the rule about children is standard for all dogs, Malamutes, despite their history as team-oriented sled dogs, are prone to fighting with one another over food and possessions, with ugly results.

Other Animals

Through diligent attention to socialization, you might be able to squelch the Malamute's innate predatory tendencies somewhat by introducing a young puppy to other animals, too, which is especially critical if this dog will be living with cats. Savvy breeders and Malamute rescuers recommend that all Malamute puppies be socialized with cats. Malamutes raised with cats tend to be less predatory toward the feline species, which can be a benefit somewhere down the line if the dog needs to go to a new home where cats reside.

Loud Noises

Finally, enhance your socialization program by exposing the dog to everyday household noises. If your pup happens to be afraid of loud noises, introduce it gradually and positively to such sounds as a vacuum cleaner or a blender. Expose the dog to these imagined threats gradually for increas-

Even as puppies, Malamutes exhibit a strong affection for humans, an affection owners should reward by spending a great deal of time with the young dogs.

ing periods of time, and you should be able to convince the animal that it has nothing to fear. With patience and consistency, such tactics can work wonders, resulting in an easygoing dog

Alaskan Malamutes tend to have sharp predatory instincts that will send them chasing after small animals (including other pets in the household, such as hamsters and cats).

29

Although it is the quintessential sled dog of the Arctic and enjoys outdoor activities, the Malamute should be offered ample time indoors with its family, as well.

with an adventurous spirit and an enthusiastic lust for life.

Visiting the Veterinarian

Another component to socialization is introducing the puppy to the veterinarian, thus launching a relationship that will remain a constant throughout the dog's life. There will be ample opportunity to forge this relationship during the first few months when the puppy must visit the veterinarian every few weeks for its routine vaccinations and physical examinations.

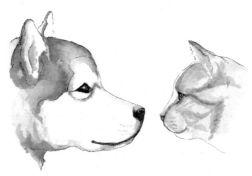

Because Alaskan Malamutes can be predatory toward small animals, socialize a puppy to cats at a young age.

By about six months of age, the puppy should also visit the veterinarian for spaying or neutering. Done early, altering can substantially reduce the incidence of various cancers later in a dog's life. But whether visiting the veterinarian for minor altering surgery, or for a quick injection, make each experience pleasurable and positive for the dog. Bring treats, and behave in an upbeat, enthusiastic manner that will help the dog build positive associations with the veterinary office. Even though it may understand that this is where "shots" occur, convince the dog through positive reinforcement that this place isn't so bad after all. A dog so convinced will be far more willing to return in the future.

Everyday Habits

Dogs are not whelped automatically understanding the adjustments they will have to make that are inherent to being a pet dog in our society. For its first few weeks of life, for example, the young puppy has no idea that soon it will be asked to walk cooperatively with its owner, led by a leash of leather or nylon. It is the owner's job to teach the pup this skill, as always with patience and positive reinforcement.

Walking on leash: Begin these lessons as early as possible, first by introducing the puppy to the collar, which it should wear at all times. Occasionally snap the leash to the collar and allow the pup to walk around the house dragging the leash behind it. Once it has grown accustomed to this, hold the leash to allow the pup to get used to that new sensation, as well. Keep all such sessions short. Rewarded with praise and treats as it masters the art of walking on leash, the dog's greatest reward will be the increased freedom it enjoys as its behavior earns it access to a wide range of locales.

Grooming: Similar early attention should be given to grooming. The earlier a puppy is introduced to brushing, bathing, ear cleaning, tooth brushing, and nail clipping, the more cooperative it will be toward these when it weighs in at 90 or 100 pounds (41–45.4 kg) and is far more capable of fighting the hand that grooms it. When grooming is introduced early and positively, the dog will also learn how pleasurable grooming time can be. As an added bonus, your dog's cooperation with your efforts reinforces the fact that you are in charge and that it must in turn lie still as you brush its tummy or clip its nails.

Introduce your puppy to a varitey of new experiences and sounds so it will grow accustomed to the great diversity of the world around it.

Toys and Games

Dogs cannot live by food and water alone. They need toys, too, and a wide variety from which to choose. Beginning with their penchant for chew toys as puppies, a necessity to help them through the teething process, most will blossom into adulthood with a healthy affection for playthings and games.

You will be wise to teach the puppy early on that some items belong to the dog and some belong to the human family members, the latter being off limits to the pooch. Make sure the dog always has access to its own collection of toys that are safe, sturdy, and free of small parts that might become casualties of vigorous play and lodge in a canine throat or intestine.

As renowned as it is for its dignity, the Malamute is equally famous for its sense of humor—it also loves games. Keep this in mind during your own games of football, baseball, Frisbee, and the like, in which you can invite your Malamute to participate. Keep control of the situation, however, and avoid such aggressive games as tug-of-war, which can overstimulate the dog

and become a test of dominance between dog and owner.

Rely on your creativity to design Malamute games. Consider hide-and-seek, for example. Upon recruiting a Malamute as your playmate, it will quickly understand that it is to wait (*stay*) while you hide. Then call it to you. With great gusto it will seek you out, its reward being that moment when it finds the person it loves most in the world hiding in a closet or behind a door.

The Boarding Kennel

There comes a time in every dog owner's life when he or she must leave home for a destination that, heaven forbid, does not allow dogs. Fortunately, in this day and age there are several options available for what to do with the dog when you are away.

While you may call in a pet sitter to feed and walk the dog at your own home several times a day, the most popular option is the boarding kennel. This may be a kennel operated by a veterinary hospital or a breeder, or one of the luxury pet hotels that now cater to the canine species. Whichever type

The full-grown Malamute is far more likely to tolerate nail clipping if it is introduced to the procedure in a positive way during puppyhood.

Few sights are as comforting as the Malamute's smile.

of kennel you choose, check out the premises ahead of time for cleanliness and space, ask about the diet and exercise that is provided, and remember that reservations are usually mandatory during holidays and other peak travel times.

A properly prepared dog should take well to kenneling, thus easing your mind when you must leave the dog behind for a few days. Introduce the dog to kenneling at a young age and prevent the separation anxiety that can afflict an older homebody who is shocked when it is sent suddenly to the kennel. You may also find comfort in that, being the lovable hunk it tends to be, your Malamute may very well become the kennel favorite, and thus receive an extra dose of attention that makes its time away from home all the more pleasant.

Understanding Alaskan Malamutes

The Importance of the Pack

There are few breeds as sensitive to the protocols of pack order as the Alaskan Malamute. From the moment this dog enters a new household, whether it is an eight-week-old puppy or a five-year-old adult, it will be unable to rest until it knows where it belongs in the family hierarchy. If you ignore the dog's need to find its place, you shirk your duties in letting it know that you are the leader, or alpha, and the Malamute will gladly accept that role for itself. This dog, even at a very young age, will recognize immediately if you vacillate or are in any way unsure in your resolve, and it will take advantage of the opportunity.

But just how do you assert your role as leader to this potentially domineering and very large dog? Some believe that physical punishment and cruelty are the answer. They're not. Treatment of that sort will only foster a timid or overly aggressive Malamute that in every way violates what this dog and its bond to the human species are meant to be.

The answer is far less traumatic. Remain firm, patient, and consistent in your interactions with the dog, and you will succeed not only in convincing it that you are the boss, but you will do

If offered the optimum mix of love and discipline, Alaskan Malamutes bond deeply with their owners and become beloved members of the family.

As they grow, young puppies learn how to be dogs by interacting with their littermates.

this via a method the dog will naturally understand. When you give a command, insist that the dog obey it. At bedtime, make sure it understands, every single night without exception, that you have your bed and the dog has its bed. If the dog decides it wants to jump up on you (a potential hazard when it hits the 90-pound [41 kg] mark), let it know, with a loud *"Off"* or *"Down"* and a step backward, that it will never be allowed.

In time, this extremely intelligent, sensitive animal will realize that you are the leader. Period. The dog may continue to challenge and test you just to make sure you really mean it, but when it does, your response must be the same—consistently. You must not waver. Remain true to this mission and you will be rewarded with a dog that is content and confident in knowing that this is its pack and this is its place in it.

While the mechanics of establishing the family pack sound simple enough, many owners, especially when faced with an adorable puppy that simply wants to wiggle and play and lick the faces of its family, decide that the training can wait. But the puppy's mother doesn't see it that way. She begins to mold the character of her pups immediately, and now you must take over that responsibility for her,

whether you are dealing with a young puppy or a mature adult Malamute.

The Stages of Development

As a dog matures, it travels through different stages of development, most of which closely resemble the stages of human development. Recognizing and understanding those stages will help you better deal with and appreciate this great animal through all its wondrous transitions.

Puppyhood

The puppy comes into the world blind, relatively immobile, completely helpless. A fledgling predator, it relies during its first few weeks of life on its mother's care. She is its source of food, warmth, and survival. Then, at about four or five weeks of age, its eyes open, it takes notice of the world, and makes primitive attempts to interact both with its littermates and other treasures in its environment. It may initiate games of tug-of-war with a sister or chew happily on a brother's ear, all the while venturing further and further from the safety and security of Mom. Yet she is never far, ready to intervene in order to instruct her young on the do's and don'ts of acceptable behavior.

At about eight weeks of age, the puppy is weaned and, assuming Mom was nurturing and attentive, ready emotionally to make the leap to a new human family. Once installed in its new home, the puppy should continue to be instructed in manners and deportment, now by its human mom. Through its first few months it will joyfully follow you from room to room, eagerly learning who is who in the family pack, mastering the ropes of housebreaking, and even beginning to learn the basic commands.

Adolescence

Somewhere between four and six months of age, the puppy will enter adolescence. Physically it will lose that soft puppy coat, and its ears will suddenly seem too large for its head, its legs too long for its body. But even more striking is the fact that the once sweet, willing, and attentive puppy will suddenly begin to ignore its owner's requests and will seem to have forgotten all it has learned to this point. Anyone who has witnessed or experienced human adolescence is well aware of the symptoms.

Adolescence can be a challenging time for the owner of the growing Malamute. As the dog attempts to assert itself, the owner may wonder why he or she ever thought getting a dog was a good idea. Indeed, frustration can lend an unpleasant aura to the relationship, but stick with it and remain consistent and firm. The young dog will ultimately acquiesce, understanding that you obviously mean business.

Try and look at the bright side. This is a time of great physical development, during which you suddenly see that yes, this is going to be a large, athletic dog. While it may be guided by a stubborn streak at the moment, it is also thrilled to be invited to participate in new games and activities—longer walks, preliminary sledding exercises, and so on—that were not appropriate for a young puppy. By sharing these experiences, you may channel those abundant adolescent energies into positive directions, and continue to forge the strong foundation upon which your relationship will rest in the future. In the meantime, keep your sense of humor. This, too, shall pass.

Maturity

Because it is a large breed, the Alaskan Malamute may take longer to mature than will its smaller counterparts. It may not fill out fully until about two years of age, and its mental development may take even longer. The young adult Malamute should be exu-

berant and active. Even if you have remained consistent in its training, its *joie de vivre* may still get the best of it at times; however, it should be more settled, and yes, cooperative, than it was as an adolescent.

By age five or six, the Malamute that has enjoyed proper training and care should be well settled into maturity. The dog has finally made it through its formative stages, it knows who it is, and it wants nothing more than to live as companion and partner to its human family members. Some of the breed's enthusiasts think this is the ideal age to bring a new Malamute into the family, considering the mature Alaskan Malamute to be one of the finest pets dogdom has to offer—to, as we've seen, the appropriate owner, of course.

A Positive Approach

Just as owners must pledge to remain consistent in their treatment of their Alaskan Malamute, so must they simultaneously commit to a positive philosophy of training. Harsh physical or otherwise negative training methods require more effort and reap poor results.

The Malamute is a sensitive animal that, though stubborn at times, will understand very quickly what is being asked of it. It may just require a bit of convincing to comply. Making training a positive, fun, and interesting activity can help to accomplish this.

Trained via positive reinforcement, the dog learns that there are pleasant rewards for behaving in certain ways. It is motivated to perform or to behave, not by fear, pain, or threats, but by the rewards it enjoys from doing so. This begins when it learns it will be praised profusely for not eliminating on the living room carpet, but out in the backyard. It learns to sit on command because this pleases its owner, evident in the fact that it also receives a favored treat when it obeys the command. It learns

As they begin to venture away from their mother, puppies learn about the world and dog behavior by interacting with their littermates.

Although Malamutes are considered terrible watchdogs, few would-be attackers are likely to approach someone with so large a dog by his or her side.

to walk on a leash because that means it gets to go out and explore the world.

Such a focus on all that is positive can even help correct annoying habits. Behaviorist William Campbell, who has employed this philosophy quite successfully, recommends that owners use what he calls the "jolly routine." Imagine that you have a dog that barks at the postal carrier each day. When you spot the innocent victim coming up the walk, attract your dog's attention by behaving in a silly, "jolly" way: Tickle the dog, praise the dog, be the clown. In time, the dog will associate the postal carrier's arrival with your joyful behavior and no longer feel the need to bark.

Training with a positive focus is not only a more humane way to go, but is far more pleasant—and safe—for the owner. How rewarding to know that one need not physically punish or react angrily to a dog for it to progress. In fact, if you choose the negative path, you are likely to make no progress at all with the Malamute, a dog that has no patience for disrespectful treatment or arbitrary, unjust punishments.

Even for the people-loving Malamute, part of every puppy's basic education should include socialization to a wide variety of people and experiences.

Even dog trainers have been known to label the headstrong, independent Malamute as "stupid." When seeking a trainer, find one who understands and respects the breed and has had experience working with such a dog.

HOW-TO:
The Basic Commands

What follows are the basic commands that every dog should know and one method you can use to teach them. Once the dog has mastered these, it may expand its repertoire—and its vocabulary—into such commands as *"Shake"* (as in to "shake" paws), *"Roll over,"* and *"Speak,"* and of course the various commands associated with mushing and similarly athletic activities.

Sit

When using the treat-reward system to teach the *sit,* the first and simplest command to teach, you can use a treat to "trick" the puppy into sitting.

Hold a treat up above the head of a standing malamute and move your hand backward. The dog will automatically follow the moving treat with its head and suddenly find itself in a sitting position.

The proper way to place a choke collar on a dog. Note the backward "6" shape.

Approach the standing puppy and show it the treat in your hand. Move the treat back up over the puppy's head while saying *"Sit."* As the puppy follows the treat with its eyes and its nose, it suddenly finds it is sitting. Praise the pup and give it its reward.

Down

Place the dog in a *sit* and again, tantalize it with the treat in your hand. Once it's attention is on the treat held near its nose, move your hand slowly and vertically down to the floor while issuing the *down* command. The dog will naturally follow the treat down to the point where it is lying on the ground, for which it will receive both praise and the treat as its reward.

Stay/Come

Stay and *come* are most easily taught together. First, with the dog in a *sit,* back away slowly while giving the *stay* command. Move back only a short distance, say the command again, then return slowly to the dog and praise and reward it for having stayed put. Gradually lengthen the distance you move back, and soon the dog will not have any doubt what *"Stay"* means.

Once the dog seems to have mastered the *stay,* you can add the *come.* After you have backed away and praised the dog verbally for staying, issue the *come* command. You may have to embellish it by slapping your thigh and calling the dog to you in a joyful, playful voice. If all else fails, offer a treat, anything to let the dog know that you want it to come to you. When it does, praise and rewards are in order. Once the dog understands the command, you should be able to replace the happy routine with a simple *come* command.

Come is an important command because, even though your dog should not be out and about off leash, there may be times when you need to call it to you, and it's comforting to think that it will indeed obey. When practicing, if the dog refuses, or simply takes its sweet time in getting over to you, resist the temptation to scold or punish the dog when it finally obeys. This will confuse the dog—it came to you, however slowly, when you called it, only to be punished. If you intend to scold the dog for noncompliance, go to the dog instead of calling it to you. Malamutes are too smart to come willingly for a scolding. Remain consistent and clear in your messages.

Heel

As large sled dogs that are bred and born to pull, heeling

does not necessarily come naturally to the Malamute. Frankly, some trainers do not even see the need for a dog to walk perfectly at your heels, preferring instead to see a dog that is free to explore without pulling on the leash and dragging an unwitting owner down the sidewalk, causing a downright dangerous situation.

Hand signals used in conjunction with vocal commands can make the training and the learning all the more effective.

A dog in a perfect *heel* walks to the left of its owner, the leash loose and hanging in the shape of a J. With much work, you might get a Malamute to fit this picture, but for most owners, just getting the dog not to pull will suffice. Again, treats can come in handy here, holding the treat down at your side to attract the dog's attention, and praising it for walking without pulling.

You can also try this exercise: Walk forward with the dog and then suddenly do an about-face, either to the side or to the rear. This will pull the dog into a new direction and perhaps startle it. Do this several times (with praise and rewards, of course), and soon the dog will understand that it should be watching you to see what you might do. In so doing, it refrains from pulling on the leash and becomes more attentive to the person at the other end.

Fetch

In teaching this ever-popular play command, toss a favorite toy, and command the dog to *fetch* it. Once it complies, call the dog enthusiastically back to you. When it returns to you, the dog may not understand that it should then give the item to you. Convince it to do so, perhaps by offering it a treat as a replacement and by using the command *Drop it.* This can turn into an enjoyable game for all involved, and it may ultimately blossom into a handy household skill, as well. For example, if you are doing laundry and drop a sock en route from the hamper to the washer, just ask the dog to *fetch* it and bring it to you for washing. The dog—a working breed, remember—will be pleased to help, or pleased to take the sock and run. It all depends on its sense of humor at the moment.

If you don't intend to show your dog in conformation, it may not need to learn the perfect heel. *Simply learning to walk nicely on the leash without pulling is sufficient for most pet Malamutes.*

Puppy Kindergarten

Not too long ago, the standard practice was to wait until a puppy reached six months of age before beginning its formal training. But as we've seen, its mom begins right away, and so should we.

This philosophy has been institutionalized in the past decade or so in the emergence of a special type of puppy training class referred to as "puppy kindergarten." Welcoming puppies as young as three months of age (who have had most of their vaccinations), these classes promote socialization and introduce the young students to basic commands.

Each class typically begins with a play session, during which the puppies have the opportunity to wrestle and

At times it seems that the Alaskan Malamute, a decidedly independent animal, chooses to listen to its own drummer, rather than obey the commands of its owner.

tumble together. While this helps the puppies expend the excess energy that could interrupt their concentration once the formal part of class begins, so does it introduce them to other puppies of all sizes, shapes, and colors, teaching them that other dogs are to be playmates not opponents.

Once the play session is over, school begins. The trick to teaching young puppies is to keep the sessions short, lively, and rich with treat rewards that keep the puppies' attention. Most newcomers to puppy kindergarten class are amazed at how fascinated young puppies can be with the mechanics of such a formally structured class, and how quickly and willingly they can learn to sit, lie down, stay, and come on command. Educated as youngsters, they will be far more successful students later when they enter a more traditional obedience class designed for older puppies. They will be better pets at

The sensitive, though headstrong, Malamute will respond best to consistent, and very positive, training methods.

home, too, for training of this type reinforces your role as leader and the puppy's role as partner, teammate, and companion.

While you may employ the tenets of puppy kindergarten training at home on your own—and you must hold short homework sessions each day between classes to reinforce the lessons—the class environment is superior because of the socialization factor.

Finding the Proper Trainer

It takes a village to raise a Malamute properly. That is how it has always been since the days when the dogs literally lived in Inuit villages in the Arctic, and it remains true today. This gregarious, people-loving dog's contemporary village is comprised first of the breeder who takes great care in bringing it into the world, followed by the carefully chosen owners who become the dog's home pack, and finally by the trainers who will instruct it in its basic manners and in the skills necessary for such activities as mushing or weight pulling should you decide you would like to see your dog participate in those traditional pursuits.

While it would indeed be a perfect world if all dogs were enrolled in obedience classes, this is especially critical for the Alaskan Malamute. Although they may not typically meet the criteria required for the obedience show ring, Malamutes do require training to give them a sense of structure and security. Attend obedience classes throughout the Malamute's first two years of life—or for the first year or two after an adult Malamute joins your family. Working together this way not only teaches the dog basic commands, but also strengthens the bond between the dog and its owner.

Many a Malamute owner has been told by professional dog trainers that this breed is "stupid." That is not true, of course, but to those accustomed only to working with very obedient

An Alaskan Malamute can easily learn the basic obedience commands, but training sessions should remain relatively short to prevent this intelligent dog from becoming bored.

Golden Retrievers and the like, one might indeed be likely to chalk the Malamute's independent character up to a lack of intelligence. Consequently, finding the right trainer to populate your Malamute's village may take more effort than would finding one for more willing a student.

What to Look For

When seeking a trainer for your Malamute, look for someone who has experience working with this breed—or at least with some type of large, strong-willed dog, ideally of the Nordic variety. Avoid the trainer who bashes the breed for its lack of brains, who prescribes to obsolete, not to mention counterproductive, force-training methods, or who cringes during an initial meeting when you mention your dog's breed. A superior candidate is that individual who smiles at the name of the breed and relishes the challenge of working with such a dog. Another good sign is the trainer who would prefer that the whole family attend the class to ensure that all are properly

A choke collar is most effective when positioned correctly on the dog. The chain collar on the left is positioned correctly; the collar on the right is incorrect.

prepared to guide and interact effectively with this unique animal.

In addition to evaluating a prospective trainer's Malamute IQ, ask about his or her training philosophy and methods. You have a vested interest in how your dog will be treated, and if you suspect the methods employed will be too harsh for your or your dog's liking, or if you sense the trainer is looking for shortcuts, perhaps with gimmicky gadgets, such as prong collars on young puppies, rather than pursuing solid,

The dog should wear a traditional buckle collar in nylon or leather at all times, but you may wish to employ a choke style collar for training.

permanent teaching and behavior modification, look elsewhere.

And finally, determine if you are compatible with the trainer, too. Dog training classes are essentially designed more for the training of the owner than of the dog, for once the class is over, it's up to the owner to continue and reinforce the lessons. If you are uncomfortable with the trainer, you probably won't learn as effectively as you might with someone who sets you at ease.

Training Tenets

Positive reinforcement: As sharp as they are, Malamutes are quick to master any number of skills, yet most training finds its roots in the fundamentals of obedience. A variety of methods exist on how best to train, but in keeping with the tenets of positive reinforcement, it's usually more effective to encourage the dog to do what you want it to do rather than punishing it for what you don't want it to do. You will probably find it easiest to reward the dog with treats, to keep the training sessions short and interesting, and to set aside time every day for training. And ignore the myth that you can't teach an old dog new tricks. You can teach any dog new tricks, as most find working with their owners in this way quite rewarding. You may just have to be more patient with the older dog that is more likely to be set in its ways.

Special training collars: You may also find it effective to use a special collar for training, perhaps a chain training collar (this is preferable to the prong collar, which is unnecessary for most dogs, and painful when employed by unskilled novices). The chain collar should not be used on puppies younger than six months of age whose neck muscles might not yet be fully developed, and it should be used for training or walking only; if you use it as the dog's everyday collar, the dog might choke or hang itself. When the dog sees you approach with the collar, it will know that it's time for training.

The chain training collar must be placed on the dog correctly for optimum comfort and results. Fit the chain through an end ring, forming a loop. When facing the dog, hold the collar's loop open; it should be the shape of a backward "6." Place it over the dog's head. Correctly positioned on a dog that is walking on your left side, the chain will tighten when you pull on the leash, and loosen automatically when you release that pressure.

An enclosed area: Choose an enclosed area for training that is far from such distractions as baseball games or a traffic-filled street.

Some training methods require that you pull or push the dog into the proper positions with a training collar and your hands. But if you refrain from touching the dog, its training might stick more effectively because the dog is more inclined to believe that its actions are its own idea. Above all, remember that you must never lose your temper. Sometimes it can take days to convince a Malamute to comply with your requests, but remain calm, firm, patient, and consistent. If the dog is distracted or refuses to cooperate, have it obey one more command, end the session, and resume when you are both more amenable to working.

A Positive Look at Behavior Problems

Every year, millions of dogs, including Alaskan Malamutes, are dispatched to the nation's animal shelters because they have developed behavioral problems that their owners are either unwilling or unable to correct. In most cases, with just a little bit of attention from a skilled behaviorist and a committed owner, such dogs can learn to recognize the error of their ways and act to preserve their place in the family—and perhaps save their lives.

The major problems that lead to such a tragic end are incessant barking (or, in the case of the Malamute, incessant howling), digging, chewing, and aggression. In virtually every case where a behavior problem leads to the premature dissolution of the dog/owner relationship, there is a reason for the dog's behavior. When that dog is a large, robust Malamute, the result can be massive destruction—perhaps ruining a wall or a carved wooden banister—for which the unwitting owner was totally unprepared. In most such cases, the problem can be remedied, simply by recognizing the underlying cause and directing the dog's attention and energy in more positive directions.

Barking: That barking dog, for instance, is most likely lonely, the unwitting victim of perhaps well-meaning owners who don't realize that they cannot just keep the dog in the yard day in and day out with little or no companionship and even less exercise. Such a dog is in need of more attention from and activity with its family, and perhaps a large canine companion of the opposite gender, as well.

Chewing: As for the Olympian chewer, it is usually a younger dog that is experiencing the irritation of teething and is lacking a sufficient collection of appropriate chew toys. It thus relieves the irritation on table legs, leather shoes, or anything it finds. A lonely or similarly unhappy adult dog may also resort to chewing, doing a great deal of damage in the process. This dog, too, needs more activity in its life, and plenty of safe and sturdy chew toys on which to vent its pent-up energies and aggressions.

Digging: Employ a similar tactic in the handling of the dog that digs, which many a Malamute does either out of

Puppies must have an ample supply of chew toys available to help relieve the discomfort of teething.

The Malamute's mind must be exercised just as diligently as its body to prevent such behavior problems as inappropriate digging, chewing, and barking.

Children and Malamutes are a natural combination, but they must never be left unsupervised.

frustration or the sheer joy of it. Here again the dog may need more exercise and companionship. You may also satisfy the dog's cravings by providing it with a section of the yard that it can dig up to its heart's content. Bury toys or bones in the Malamute digging pit to teach it that this is its special spot, and if the dog begins digging elsewhere, move it to the legal area and encourage it to go at it. Remember, when faced with behavior problems, providing alternatives and channeling the dog's energies in more positive directions is far superior to, and more productive than, punishment.

Aggression: The overly aggressive dog is potentially dangerous, especially if its aggression is directed toward family members. There are many reasons for such tendencies, and most cases are best addressed with the help of an experienced canine behaviorist. He or she is best able to diagnose the cause and prescribe the proper therapy for correcting the problem. But, sadly, sometimes the situation has gone too far, the dog is too severely affected, and the safest remedy is euthanasia.

Kids and Malamutes

For centuries Malamutes have held a special affinity for children, and the feelings are mutual. Still, you must exercise the same caution you would with any dog when children are involved. Namely, never leave the dog, even the most trustworthy Malamute, alone and unattended with children, and make the effort to teach your kids how to behave around dogs—both their own and others they meet on the street.

It is not unusual today to be out on a walk with a dog and be accosted by children who run toward you screaming in their delight to see "the doggie." These children have not been taught how to approach strange dogs and will probably soon be added to the ever-growing list of America's dog-bite casualties.

On the flip side is the child who quietly approaches and asks to pet your

If your Malamute enjoys digging—as most do—provide it with its own corner of the yard in which to do so, and make sure it gets plenty of exercise to ensure its behavior is not a manifestation of loneliness or boredom.

dog. This child, having been taught appropriate manners, usually knows to allow the dog to sniff his or her hand first. The child then pets the dog on the shoulder or side where the animal can monitor his or her movements,

Alaskan Malamutes have always shared a special bond with children, but children should be taught how to handle the dog with gentleness and respect.

rather than patting it on the top of the head, out of the dog's field of vision. Teaching your children these protocols, as well as how to care for and handle their own puppies and dogs properly, will ensure that they will not be party to a dog-bite event, many of which are more the fault of the children (and thus the parents) than they are of the dog.

The New Baby and the Malamute

Other related mistakes occur when owners bring a new baby into a home with a resident dog who has long occupied an important niche in the family pack. Far too many new parents mistakenly believe that now that a child is around, the dog must be exiled to the backyard. The dog in turn grows resentful of the child, to whom it may not have even been formally introduced. A more productive tact is to make the dog a part of the baby's life from the very beginning. Introduce it to the small bundle as soon as you bring the baby home. Allow the dog to grow accustomed to the newcomer's scent and to accompany you when it's time for feedings, diaper changes, baths, and walks.

As with all new experiences, make the baby's arrival as positive as possible for the dog. That way, as the baby grows and enters those more challenging stages of crawling and of grabbing handfuls of Malamute hair, the dog will be bonded to the child and perhaps be more forgiving. Nevertheless, make sure that all interactions between the two are closely monitored at all times to prevent and avoid mishap, and never force the dog to be with the child in an enclosed space, such as a bedroom, or—heaven forbid—a crib or playpen. Allow the dog to decide for itself when it wants to be near the child, and give it time to build its own relationship, one that should blossom into something beautiful as the child comes to know and love its pet Malamute.

Feeding
a Very Large Dog

The History of
Malamute Feeding

When one beholds the vision that is the healthy Alaskan Malamute, the signs are unmistakable. The dog walks with confidence in its step, propelled forward by a combination of strong, hard bones and powerful muscles. Its eyes are clear and bright, its coat thick and lustrous. This dog is obviously receiving a diet rich in the high-quality nutrients it needs to cut that figure of energy and health.

Nutrition is a relatively new concern in canine care. Historically, throughout most of their domestic relationship with humans, dogs typically received our leftovers. They may have helped their humans track and hunt their prey, but generally to the humans went the bulk of the spoils. This pattern was particularly evident among Arctic sled dogs that would share their people's food, yet receive just enough to fuel their rigorous winter duties on the snow and ice, their rations then cut back severely during summer "vacation" to an amount just enough to keep them alive.

Although the Arctic people, as well as others throughout the world who lived with dogs, understood that canine performance depended on fuel, few consciously worried about balance or nutrients. Even a few decades ago, with only a handful of brands of commercial dog foods on the market, dog owners rarely gave a thought to what might be in that can or in that bag. Even veterinary schools devoted very little time to the importance of nutrition.

Times have changed substantially since the dark ages of canine nutrition. We now know that the content and quality of the foods that go into the dog to nourish it internally will eventually make themselves evident externally in the dog's appearance, behavior, and performance. Because we have come to realize that nutrition offers us an easy barometer of canine health, it is getting a lot more respect these days, evident in the high-quality commercial foods now available not only to satisfy our dogs' appetites, but to help them enjoy optimum health and longevity.

Basic Nutritional
Building Blocks

Despite how it might look at first glance, dogs are not true carnivores. They, like us, are omnivores, meaning they fare best on a ration comprised of both meat and vegetable material. If you opt to feed the domestic dog nothing but meat, the detrimental effects of this will become quickly apparent in the dog's coat, its eyes, its entire demeanor.

This may seem a puzzling concept considering that the domestic dog occupies only one branch of a large canid family tree, whose other branches house such wild, profoundly meat-eating dogs as wolves, foxes, coyotes, and the like. But, as wildlife biologists know, even these wild meat eaters relish some vegetation in their diets, collected from the digestive tracts of their herbivorous prey.

The magical combination of animal and vegetable material offers the dog the full complement of nutrients it requires. These include proteins, fats, carbohydrates, vitamins, minerals, and water, each of which plays a critical role in the operation of the dog's system.

Protein

Whether derived from plant or animal sources, protein is a fundamental building block of the canine diet; but all proteins are not created equal, and herein lies the challenge.

With commercial dog foods, you often get what you pay for. If you seek the least expensive brand, you will probably also wind up with the poorest quality protein, thus sacrificing the health of the dog's bones, muscle, blood, and countless other tissues and organs. While the dog's protein needs will change during the course of its life, the young puppy and the high-powered athlete requiring more protein than the sedentary senior, all need the highest-quality protein, and none can afford the physical degeneration poor-quality food can cause.

Fats

Despite its bad press, fat is an essential nutrient in the canine diet, required to fuel the dog's energy needs, which, for a working Malamute, can be substantial. As with protein, fat needs will differ from dog to dog, depending on age and career (e.g., sled dog, weight puller, etc.). But whether the dietary fat comes from either plant or animal sources, overnourishing a dog, any dog, with fat (most commonly accomplished by plying the dog with table scraps from the human dinner table) will lead to a fat dog and yet another contribution to the serious obesity problem in America's canine population.

Carbohydrates

A dog's energy needs are not fueled by fats alone. Assisting them in this job are carbohydrates, although carbos are not typically as high in energy as are fats. Carbohydrates are prominent players in most commercial dog food formulations, present in such key ingredients as corn, rice, and barley. They play an important role in both the working Malamute's ability to travel long distances over the ice and snow, and the companion Malamute's afternoon spent competing in agility.

Vitamins and Minerals

A great many dog owners succumb to the advertising promises that particular vitamin and/or mineral supplements are what dogs need for complete and balanced nutrition. This, however, is not true if the dog is receiving one of the high-quality, "complete and balanced" commercial dog foods currently on the market. What all dog owners are wise to realize is that oversupplementing dogs can be just as damaging as undernourishing them. We must fight that natural human inclination that holds if a little is good, more must surely be better.

That "more" can be dangerous if the vitamins being supplemented are the fat-soluble A or D. Unlike the water-soluble Bs and C (the latter of which some breeders supplement to enhance calcium metabolism in Malamutes), which are flushed through the body each day, vitamins A and D accumulate in the tissues and end up preventing the beneficial functions they are meant to facilitate.

Minerals as supplements can also bring negative results. Consider, for instance, calcium, a mineral instrumental in bone growth. If you decide that your dog should have more calcium in its diet, you will throw phosphorus off kilter, as the two must be balanced to perform their duties properly. You are better off leaving the chemistry to the experts and reaping the benefits of their research by feeding your dog a high-quality commercial diet that fits the "complete and balanced" criteria.

Fish as a supplement: There is, however, one type of "supplement" that some Malamute breeders have come to recommend. Looking to the history of their breed, and hence to its historically fish-heavy diet, which was radically changed to grain-based nutrition as soon as the dog was brought down into the lower 48 states, some have suspected that perhaps a weekly supplemental ration of fish (say, one-quarter of a can of mackerel) would provide their dogs with a more Malamute-friendly form of iodine. This is not simply breeder folklore either, as selected manufacturers of commercial pet foods have begun to add fish oil to some of their foods to enhance coat and skin health, an addition devotees of Nordic breeds see as a positive step for their dogs.

Water

One may not expect to find water included in a list of dietary building blocks for dogs, but without the presence of simple H_2O each and every day, none of the other nutrients can be metabolized or transported throughout the body. In fact, water is itself the prime component of the dog's body (as well as the human's), thus creating the demand for a steady stream of it to ensure that the biological system has the supply it needs for optimum performance.

Unfortunately, Malamutes don't always care to drink when they should, especially when the mercury dips below the freezing point on a frosty morning, and the Malamute team is anxious to take off pulling a sled through the snow. However, these dogs, as well as any dog about to embark on a demanding activity, must lap up an ample supply of water before they begin.

The Alaskan Malamute must have ample supplies of cool, clean, fresh water available at all times, winter and summer.

Take a hint from mushers who know: Spike the water with some sort of irresistible flavoring agent (unsalted meat broth or stock of some kind is always a favorite). No self-respecting dog can turn down such a treat, and no self-respecting owner should allow any dog ever to face an empty water dish, whether the temperature is 90°F (32°C) in California, or 10 below (−18°C) in Alaska.

What to Feed

So you have committed yourself to providing your Malamute with a healthy, well-balanced diet, only to find that there are now hundreds of brands of foods on the market. You cannot simply close your eyes and choose, because just as proteins are not all created equal, neither are all the dog foods that contain those many proteins.

An Easy Transition

The first step toward choosing the brand of dog food is to consult your dog's breeder or previous caretaker. For the first few days or weeks the

49

puppy or dog should receive what it was fed before it came into your household (assuming, of course, that you consider it an acceptable product), even if that is not what you would like to see it eat in the future.

Having remained true to your dog's previous diet upon first bringing the animal, puppy or adult, into your home, once you believe the time is right to switch the dog over to its new food, do so gradually over the course of several days. Each day, mix more and more of the new food in with the old until finally the entire dish is filled with the new food. This way your dog need not suffer the gastric upset a sudden change can cause, especially during what can be a very emotionally trying time for the dog.

Labeling

The next tool you may use in choosing your dog's food is the label on the package, but even this can be confusing if you don't know what to look for. On the positive side of this quandary, you can usually assume that if you go with a well-known brand, you will not be harming your dog. These foods are

Commercial dog foods come in dry, canned, and semimoist forms.

formulated by teams of veterinary nutritionists and scientists, who have invested a great deal of time, money, and effort into determining what dogs need nutritionally and formulating foods to meet those needs. By learning to decipher the labels, you can decide whether a food you are considering falls into this category.

By law, a dog food's label must include several key components:
• It must indicate the name of the species for which the food is intended.
• It must include a guaranteed analysis of the crude protein, crude fat, crude fiber, and moisture content of the food.
• It must offer an ingredients list that spells out ingredients in descending order of content.
• It must carry a nutritional "mission" statement, such as "complete and balanced for all life stages," or "complete and balanced for growth."

But we must look between the lines to determine the quality of the ingredients—especially of the proteins—and this is where a little knowledge can help. Specifically, look for a statement about Association of American Feed Control Officials protocols on the package, and you're on the right track.

While the simple words "beef" or "chicken by-products" on a label won't tell you much about the quality of those ingredients, a statement about AAFCO standards can. The AAFCO sets minimum and maximum nutritional guidelines for pet foods, so look for a food that states it meets those standards, and does so through the test feeding of dogs. Any reputable manufacturer that meets these standards through this method will be pleased to say so in black and white on its product's packaging.

Food Types

Once you have chosen the brand name, you must then decide whether to feed your dog dry food, semimoist patties, canned food, or a combination.

Dry kibble is by far the most popular type of dog food, and it can handily nourish a dog when offered as the animal's exclusive diet. When of a high-quality, premium variety, it is simple to feed and transport, it is relatively odor-free, and it produces firm feces that are easy to pick up and dispose of. As an added bonus, the hard consistency of dry foods, while no substitute for regular veterinary dental cleanings, can help keep the dog's teeth clean between veterinary cleaning sessions.

Semimoist foods are not typically recommended by breeders and veterinarians as the optimum choice because they can contain colorings and additives that a dog doesn't need, plus their soft texture offers no therapeutic value to the maintenance of the dog's teeth. This latter point could also be made about traditional canned dog foods, but canned foods do tend to find favor among owners who like to make their dogs' dry kibble a bit more appetizing by mixing canned food with the dry for a tasty meal. When the bulk of the diet is comprised of canned food, however, its odor can be offensive should the dog leave some behind after mealtime, and it makes softer, difficult-to-clean stools.

Special Needs, Special Foods

Just as the quality of commercial dog foods has made leaps and bounds in past years, so have the choices expanded significantly. Today, there are foods for every canine need available at pet supply stores, grocery stores, veterinary offices, and feed stores.

Puppies

Within its first year or so of life, the young Alaskan Malamute could gain 60, 70, even 80 pounds (27, 32, 36 kg) as it travels down that arduous path toward adulthood. Not only will it

Puppies require a diet higher in energy and nutrients than that designed for adult dogs.

grow at a rate that seems almost supernatural, but it will also play vigorously during its waking hours. It will therefore require more energy from its diet than will the adult Malamute who acts as world class companion rather than world class growing adolescent.

To nourish this hungry puppy, feed the youngster a complete and balanced puppy food that should comprise the bulk of its diet until it reaches 18 months or even two years of age. Don't fall into the trap, however, of believing that this large puppy requires mega-doses of nutrients. That philosophy can lead to bone disease, a common problem in overnourished large-breed puppies that are encouraged nutritionally to grow faster than they should. You must also not allow adult dogs in the house to share the puppy's rations. They will end up overnourished and possibly overweight, which isn't good for any dog.

Older Dogs/Overweight Dogs

Special foods directed toward both older and overweight dogs contain less fat and thus less energy than do regular canine maintenance diets. A food with less fat but sufficient bulk and flavor can help an overweight dog lose some of that weight and prevent a svelte senior citizen from putting on pounds that will tax its aging system. Foods for older dogs also contain less

Puppies relish their first introductions to solid food, viewing meal-times as a source of fun as well as nourishment.

winter, if your Malamute is a gainfully employed sled dog, increase the daily ration and make sure it meets all of the dog's needs. Then, after the spring thaw, assuming you have not substituted sledding with some other activity of equal physical demands, cut back on the ration to prevent the pitfalls of overnutrition. You may even find that the dog cuts back on its own, reading its own internal signals about what it does and does not need nutritionally.

Ailing Dogs

Dogs with kidney problems, dogs with allergies, dogs with digestive ailments—today there is a broad spectrum of diets available to help dogs, through nutritional means, deal with the troubles that threaten their health. The very existence of these so-called prescription diets, so named because they are available only from veterinarians, is a testament to how far we have come in our respect for nutrition in our dogs' lives and the valuable tool it provides us in maintaining our pets' health.

Feeding Strategies

How you feed your dog can be just as important as *what* you feed it. For the most part, Malamutes, natural dogs that they are, are considered easy keepers, their evolution in the Arctic having molded their metabolisms into efficient systems that will typically thrive on less food than one might expect for so large a dog. The daily ration for the Malamute, however, will depend on the individual dog, and it can vary anywhere from two cups of dry food a day to six. You can learn where in this range your dog falls by paying close attention to its eating habits, gauging its weight and conformation, and consulting with the dog's breeder and veterinarian.

In addition to determining *how much* your dog should be eating is the ques-

protein, the assumption being that a decrease in protein will reduce strain on the dog's kidneys. Should you decide to switch your dog to a geriatric diet, you may start as early as seven years of age. Should you decide your pup is overweight and needs a low-calorie, low-fat ration, start today.

Active Dogs

A Malamute who takes daily walks or runs with its owner, or who occasionally accompanies the family on day hikes or backpacking trips, can fare just fine on a high-quality canine maintenance diet. But dogs whose days include rigorous athletic conditioning for such activities as pulling a sled, weight pulling, or skijoring (see page 89), may require an extra boost of energy and nutrients. This dog is the ideal candidate for one of the high-energy diets now available.

The owner of such a dog, however, is wise to heed an important lesson from the Arctic people who would reduce their dogs' rations during the summer when their energy needs were not as high as they were in the winter. In other words, during the

tion of *how* to feed your pet. It seems so simple, yet opinions vary widely on this. The best option for a particular owner and a particular dog usually depends on which strategy meshes with the owner's lifestyle and schedule and is more comfortable for the dog.

For instance, your dog may be one of those wonders who truly looks at food as fuel and can reliably free feed. Its bowl may be kept filled at all times with food (preferably dry food to prevent the odor and spoilage of wet food), from which it can nibble whenever it feels the need. Because Malamutes can be territorial and aggressive about food, this strategy probably won't work in a multi-dog household, and it is obviously not the best choice for gluttonous animals that must have been ever-voracious beagles in their previous lives.

A popular choice is feeding the dog its entire ration in one daily feeding. This is convenient for the owner who may not be home during the day to split the daily ration into two or three smaller feedings, but the once-a-day regimen won't work for every Malamute. Puppies, for example, cannot be fed once a day because their energy needs are enormous as they experience rapid growth that requires constant infusions of fuel.

Two or three feedings a day will better sustain a puppy, and is also the wisest choice for dogs that may be prone to canine bloat (gastric dilitation-volvulus). Bloat is common among large dogs and dogs that tend to wolf down large meals, so dividing the daily ration into several feedings can help prevent this deadly condition (see page 68).

Avoiding Poor Eating Habits

Nutrition is a powerful tool at every dog owner's disposal. With that tool you can enhance your pet's health and comfort, and possibly add years to its life, as well.

But powerful tools can have a down side, too. Where there are great benefits to be reaped on one side of the equation, there can also be great danger on the other side. As we have seen, dog foods have come a long way in the last few decades, offering our dogs carefully formulated nutrition designed to fuel their various nutritional needs, but at the same time, we are also seeing an epidemic of obesity in dogs, and the two trends walk hand in hand.

Obesity

Obesity is a sad state for a dog (or human!). The dog may genuinely enjoy wolfing down the leftovers from each family member's dinner plate, and may genuinely relish receiving its own bowl of ice cream for dessert, but to allow the dog to grow accustomed to such habits is not doing the animal any favors. Aside from the fact that poor nutrition takes a terrible toll on internal organs, an obese dog simply is not comfortable. It cannot run and play as it should, its breathing comes hard, and its movements are slow and labored. Worse yet, in allowing a dog to become obese, owners are ensuring that their days with a beloved family member will be substantially reduced. Is it worth it?

If you are unsure about whether your dog is overweight (not always easy with a thick-coated Malamute), try this test: With your dog in a standing position, run your hands down its rib cage. Do you feel the ribs? If not, it's time for a diet.

Fortunately, with the new dietary dog foods, you need not starve a dog to help it take off those extra pounds. In most cases, the success of a canine weight-loss program involves the owner's resolve more than the dog's. The dog's human family members—all of them—must learn to say "No" to those big brown eyes begging scraps

To prevent obesity and gastric upset in your pet, resist the temptation to feed it table scraps and treats better suited to human metabolism.

from the table. They must bid farewell to their own bad "treating" habits, and help build new eating and exercise habits in their pet.

Underweight

If you do the obesity rib test and do feel ribs, you should think about that result as well. Are the ribs sharp and overly defined, or do you just feel the outline of the bones as well as some surrounding tissue. If the latter is true, your dog is just right. If the former is the case, your dog is probably in need of a bit more fat and calories, but they must be offered via dog food and the

doctor's orders, not by what you have left over on the dinner table each night.

If yours is a thin dog, it may be a so-called finicky eater, but don't let this send you rushing to the pet store to stock up on every type of dog food to entice your pet to the food dish. Stick with one and avoid not only digestive upset in your dog, but finicky eating habits, as well.

Treats

And finally, whether your dog is overweight, underweight, or just right, take it easy with the treats. An overweight dog may have to cut out its usual treats, but it may find it enjoys substitute carrot or zucchini slices instead. During the holidays, you may look forward to preparing a plate of turkey, stuffing, mashed potatoes, and gravy for your pet to make for a truly memorable celebration. You may end up, however, remembering not the meal, but the fact that you had to stay up all night cleaning up the dog's diarrhea.

Instead, pop open a can of turkey dog food and offer that instead. The dog that is accustomed to dry food will consider this a grand treat, while you remain guilt-free. And skip the dessert. Such foods have absolutely no place in the canine diet—especially true of chocolate, which is poisonous gastrointestinally to dogs because of an ingredient called theobromine. Train yourself to stick to these few rules, and you should all live happily ever after.

Grooming:
The Malamute Beautiful

While it takes a special brand of individual to live successfully with the potentially domineering soul that is the Alaskan Malamute, it doesn't take much to keep that old soul looking its best. Indeed, the Arctic people who first lived with this dog were too busy just trying to stay alive than to spend much time making sure that their teams of dogs were well groomed, so fortunately for them—and today for us—this very natural breed comes graced with a coat that demands little in the way of extraordinary care.

Understanding the Coat

This is not to say that the Malamute need not be groomed or that it may be neglected and will in turn radiate as a beautiful dog. Rather, the Malamute should be groomed on a regular basis, and the more regularly this is pursued, the easier it will be to accomplish.

The first step toward grooming the Alaskan Malamute is to understand that all care in this department revolves around the dog's thick double coat, the unifying signature of every breed within the family of Nordic dogs. This coat is truly a miraculous feat of Mother Nature's engineering, embodying, as the name implies, two distinctly different coats that work together to create a dynamic, and extremely effective, whole.

Bury your fingers into the coat of a Malamute, and you will get a feel for both coats. Your fingers are first greeted by long, coarse guard hairs that may even seem a bit stiffer than you are accustomed to feeling on most dogs. Dig in deeper, down to the skin, and there you will find a new sensation, your fingers suddenly coming to rest on a bed of soft, downlike fluff— the undercoat. Through this simple act, you have just discovered why this breed has so successfully thrived in some of the most extremely frigid climates and conditions this planet has to offer. It's all in the coat.

Working together, the dog's outer guard hairs and soft, fluffy undercoat are able to trap air close to the dog's body and warm it with its own body heat. As dense as the coat is—and assuming the dog has not fallen through the ice into a freezing body of water—the coat is also able to keep dangerous moisture at bay. As moisture from ice, snow, or rain clings to the outermost tips of the guard hairs, it is unable to slide down toward the undercoat where it might saturate that soft fluff and then the skin, thus chilling and potentially killing the dog in freezing temperatures. As testament to this system's efficacy, you have likely seen photographs of Arctic sled dogs curled up in the snow, their coats powdered white as if dusted with confectioners' sugar, the dogs slumbering peacefully, warm and dry within their protective outer shells.

Care of the Double Coat

Needless to say, helping the Malamute care for this mantle of hair, a coat that also tends not to convey that strong and rather distinctive

The color of most Malamute coats is a combination of white and black or shades of gray.

Proper grooming of an Alaskan Malamute requires a minimum of equipment.

"doggy" odor prevalent in other breeds, is a big responsibility, but not as daunting as it may seem.

One important key is to start early. The earlier a puppy learns to tolerate the various ministrations that will come its way in the name of grooming and cleanliness, the quicker it will adjust. That will help to keep grooming sessions positive. Whether it is that occasional bath, nail clipping, or routine daily brushing, the dog should look forward to grooming, not dread it. In sharing these moments, you are on one hand reinforcing your position as leader as the dog must cooperate with you, but you are also enhancing the bond you share with your pet.

Simple maintenance will keep the Malamute beautiful and healthy from the tip of its guard hairs all the way down to its skin, one of the most important organs of the Malamute's body. Once you make coat and skin care a part of the routine, it will accustom you to what is normal for your pet. You will thus be prepared to recognize immediately if the dog develops abnormal lumps or bumps, or if its skin and coat suddenly become dry or otherwise unhealthy, which could signal an internal health problem.

Unlike such breeds as the poodle and the cocker spaniel, which require extensive and frequent grooming to keep their coats healthy and free of mats, the very natural Malamute requires no such heroic attentions. It rarely needs a bath, and haircuts are unnecessary. What it does require is an owner who enjoys brushing his or her dog on a regular basis, which can be time consuming but does not require any unattainable level of specialized skill or training.

Supplies and Techniques for Coat Care

The supplies you gather for this job may vary. Some breeders and owners use the pin brush, an oval-shaped brush with thick, metal bristles that resemble heads of pins, while others swear by the slicker, a rectangular field of fine metal bristles that can effectively remove dead hair (although some believe it also breaks the hair left behind). Regardless of the type of brush you choose, thoroughness is everything.

Sure it's simple just to run a brush superficially through the dog's hair on its back and leave it at that, but in doing so you will not address the needs of the undercoat, or, even more importantly, reach the skin, which requires stimulation both for proper circulation and for the distribution of healthy coat oils. A more effective method of brushing and removing dead hair involves first brushing against the grain, so to speak, of the hair, brushing against the direction in which the guard hairs tend to lie. This way you automatically brush the undercoat and the guard hairs simultaneously, while reaching the skin as well. When this job is done, then you may brush with the growth of the hair for a polished, finished look. Brush the dog this way anywhere from three times a week to once a day, and you will find yourself with a Malamute that can't help but command attention.

You must be careful to brush the more difficult-to-reach spots, as well, to prevent mats that must be cut out should they develop. Don't forget that hidden region under the front leg (under the elbow), and pay close attention to the haunches, the underbelly, and that soft area behind the ears, all areas that can become riddled with mats if ignored.

The rake: Another tool Malamute veterans recommend is the rake. This comes in handy particularly once or twice a year when the Malamute sheds its soft, fluffy undercoat, a process referred to as "blowing coat."

Thorough weekly brushings are usually all the Malamute requires to keep its thick double coat healthy (except once or twice a year when the undercoat "blows," at which time the dog requires daily attention to keep the shedding under control).

The old coat, having performed its duties well, sheds out to make room for the growth of a newer, fresher growth of hair. During these few weeks, typically occurring sometime in fall and/or spring, the undercoat will come out in great clumps of fluff so profuse you will find it impossible to believe that your dog was ever able to grow so much hair. But the large clumps of soft down left around the house and wherever the dog wanders are testimony to the miracle that is the Malamute double coat. The rake can help speed up this process, as can a weekly bath until the coat is fully shed.

HOW-TO:
Care of the Ears, Eyes, Feet, Nails, and Teeth

Just as you must care for the Malamute's coat on a routine basis, so do its ears, eyes, feet, and teeth require some attention themselves. Maintain them now when they are healthy, and you'll prevent problems down the line.

Ear Care

The Malamute boasts an acute hearing ability, evident in the shape of its ears. The breed is fortunate in that its prick ears are not typically candidates for the problems and infections that can affect floppy-eared dogs. The following tips will help keep them that way:
• Look inside the ears periodically to ensure they remain clean, and, more importantly, smell them, too. Get to know what your dog's healthy ear smells like so you will be able to detect an abnormal odor should one ever develop.
• To clean your dog's ears, resist the temptation to stick

Clean your Malamute's ear with a clean cotton ball dipped in mineral oil. Clean only the ear flap and avoid the delicate ear canal.

58

The paws of so active a dog as the Malamute should be examined regularly for road salt, ice balls, and foxtails that can become embedded between the toes.

cotton swabs or similarly dangerous objects into the ear canal. Restrict your ministrations to the open, visible ear flaps, cleaning them occasionally with mineral oil on a cotton ball.
• If, during the routine care of the ears, you come to suspect a problem—or if you notice your dog scratching incessantly at one ear or shaking its head violently—contact the veterinarian.

Eye Care

Like the Malamute's ears, its eyes, too, should require little care, yet remain vigilant in your observations and observe the following protocols:
• Become familiar with what the dog's eyes normally look like so you will be able to detect such abnormalities as an unusual cast to the cornea or a sudden increase in tearing.
• Clean the corners of the dog's eyes as needed with a damp washcloth. If the eyes appear red or irritated, do not

treat them with drops or medications meant for humans unless instructed by the veterinarian to do so.
• Should you notice a sudden change in the eyes, consult the veterinarian. Sometimes a simple pollen allergy can be the cause of tearing, but don't rely on do-it-yourself diagnosis and treatment. The eyes are too important for shortcuts, and sometimes serious problems elsewhere in the body manifest secondarily as changes in the eye.

Foot Care

The typical Malamute has large feet with an abundant growth of hair around the paw pads. Since feet are the foundation of athletic movement, don't neglect them as key targets of the grooming regimen:
• While conformation show exhibitors may trim the hair around the edge of the feet to refine their look, the pet Malamute should require no such grooming.
• Check the feet regularly to make sure that the thick growth of hair remains free of ice, balls of snow, salt, and mud, and that the delicate skin between the toes does not become impaled by foxtails.
• Examine and clean the feet especially carefully after any outdoor adventure; you never know what your Malamute might pick up as it runs through the snow or explores a mountain trail.

Nail Care

Most dogs don't enjoy having their nails trimmed but they should be taught, preferably as puppies, to tolerate it.

• Trim the dog's nails on a regular basis, as overgrown nails can cause pain, limping, and even infection. Depending on the dog, the nails may require trimming anywhere from every two weeks to once a month.
• Don't allow the nails to grow to the point where the toes begin to curl up when the dog stands. If your dog has its dewclaws—the nails up on the ankle that don't touch the ground and are often removed from young puppies—remember that they must be trimmed too.
• When trimming the nails, avoid the quick, the blood-rich base of the nail. With a pair of quality nail clippers designed especially for large dogs, clip only the tip of the nail and avoid the region where it darkens.
• If you do "quick" the dog, the nail will bleed profusely, so be prepared. Apply either special blood-stopping powder or a styptic pencil, both of which are available at pet supply stores. Have these supplies ready, because even the most skilled nail trimmer has been known to cut just a little too far down from time to time.

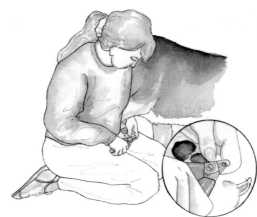

The dog will look upon nail clipping positively if you introduce it to the procedure at a young age, and take great care not to cut the sensitive, blood-rich quick at the base of the nail.

Tooth Care

With dogs now living longer than ever before, great demands are being placed on their teeth that would have been moot for dogs, say, 30 years ago. Back then and before, dogs only needed their teeth for eight, nine, maybe ten years, as that tended to be the average canine lifespan. There really was no such thing as canine gum disease, and little thought was given to the fact that dogs could develop cavities (the latter of which are more rare in dogs

than is the former). Now all that has changed, and diligent owners are wise to do all they can to help their dogs keep their teeth into their senior years. The following guidelines can assist you in this mission:
• Have the dog's teeth professionally cleaned by a veterinarian once or twice a year. Supplement this with brushing at home, ideally every day, but at least two or three times a week.

Daily toothbrushing will help your pet keep its teeth throughout its life.

• Brush your dog's teeth with a toothbrush and toothpaste specially designed for dogs (human toothpastes can cause digestive upset in dogs). These items are available at pet supply stores, as are alternatives such as finger brushes and specially coated gauze pads, which may be used on puppies or adult dogs that don't care to cooperate with traditional brushing.
• To brush your dog's teeth, proceed just as you would to brush your own teeth. Brushing in a circular pattern is an effective way to address both teeth and gums. To reach the molars in back, if the dog is amenable, place your finger into the corner of the animal's lips and pull back gently to expose the molars for brushing.
• When introducing your pet to tooth brushing, remain positive and upbeat in the hope that your attitude will prove contagious. Most dogs learn to enjoy the taste of the toothpaste and the sensation of brushing itself. They seem to understand that this must be good for them.

A seasoned show dog relaxes on the grooming table before it is called in to the ring to perform.

Bathtime Made Easier

Each Malamute is an individual. Given the breed's background and the threat immersion in water presented to Malamutes that traversed the frozen Arctic, it would seem that a fear of water would be as natural to a Malamute as an affinity to the wet stuff is to the hunting retriever. Yet, in fact, there is no universal Malamute opinion on this, and, some Malamutes love a dip in a nearby lake or swimming pool, while others avoid water like the plague. Regardless of which camp your pet happens to be part of, there comes a time in every Malamute's life, even the water-hating Malamute's life, when it must be bathed.

Without a doubt, the simplest way to bathe your dog is to have the job done by a professional groomer. Grooming shops are outfitted with all the right equipment that makes grooming so large a dog convenient or even possible. But, with a little planning, you can adapt similar techniques to accommodate your dog at home, and thus gain an immense sense of accomplishment from bathing this beautiful animal yourself. The following steps should help you in this mission.

Prepare for the Big Event

Before you even think of rounding up the dog for a bath, you must prepare. First, determine where you will be bathing the dog. This is actually possible in your own bathtub with a rubber mat on the bottom if you don't mind cleaning the bathroom from floor to ceiling afterward, but it may also be done outdoors (on a warm day, of course) in a child's wading pool, a metal washtub, or just out on the grass or patio with a hose and the dog tied to a sturdy anchor. Prepare the site ahead of time, filling the tub with lukewarm water, hooking up the hose, whatever you need to do to accommodate your water needs.

A Malamute introduced to bathing at an early age will be more amenable to the procedure as an adult.

Now gather your supplies. You will need:
- several clean, dry towels
- a shampoo formulated for dogs (perhaps a flea shampoo or one that also includes a conditioner)
- a couple of clean washcloths
- a large plastic cup to assist in rinsing
- a blow dryer (optional)

Place these all near the tub and you're ready to begin.

Splish, Splash

Because this breed is so adept at reading minds, your Malamute will probably guess before you even make a move toward preparing that you intend to give it a bath. It may begin to try and avoid you, to stay just out of reach, perhaps to disappear. Whatever you must contend with to do so, retrieve the dog and bring it to the bath. Your first challenge is to wet the dog from head to toe (or perhaps from neck to toe, some dogs being more amenable to the bath if their heads and faces can remain dry until the end). This can be a challenge because that thick double coat will fight full saturation. Spend as much time as you can in accomplishing this, and you will find the rest of the bath proceeds much more smoothly.

Now, faced with a wet dog, begin the shampooing. Just as you attempted to wet the coat down to the skin, now you will try to massage the shampoo through the hair and down to the skin, as well. In doing so, don't neglect the areas beneath the tail, the groin, behind the ears, and the profuse growth of hair at the bottom of the dog's feet.

Once the dog is sufficiently cleansed, its time to rinse. This time it's even more critical to saturate the dog completely as you must be sure to remove every bit of soap, every bubble from the dog's skin and hair. Rinse from the top of the neck and back and work your way down to the legs and feet. Then rinse, rinse, rinse again. When you no longer see soap or bubbles falling from the dog, rinse one more time. If you have reserved the washing of the dog's face and head for the end, wash the head with a drop of shampoo, the face with a clean washcloth and water, and you have successfully completed the bath.

Proper Drying

Equally important to the rinse cycle is the drying of the dog. To prevent the animal from becoming chilled, you will want to make sure it is completely dry before it runs off to resume its normal activities.

To tackle the drying of that thick double coat, begin by first patting and rubbing the dog with the clean towels you collected for this purpose, and be warned that the dog will feel compelled to help. In other words, it will insist on shaking its body from head to tail to toe as only a wet dog can do, an act that will in turn send water flying everywhere. If you are bathing outdoors, no problem. If indoors, be ready for some major post-bath cleanup.

Once the bulk of the water has been dried or shaken off, confine the dog in a warm dry spot, perhaps a corner of the kitchen, the garage, or a sheltered area outdoors to finish drying. You can accelerate the process by using a blow dryer set on warm, not hot, blowing the hair dry by directing the air against the lay of the coat (so as to dry the undercoat as well). Because the noise and sensation may startle some dogs, it is wise to introduce the animal to the blow dryer at a young age, allowing it first to explore the dryer as it sits unplugged on the floor, then introducing it to its sound, and then to the feel of the air on its coat. Most dogs, when introduced to it properly and positively, learn to enjoy being dried with the blow dryer, which can certainly help to ensure that the dog is dried all the way down to the skin.

Fighting Fleas and Ticks

Fleas

No discussion of dog grooming would be complete without mention of the seemingly neverending fight against external parasites, particularly

A close-up of the common, and difficult-to-eradicate flea.

the fight against the flea. Millions of dollars are spent each year on flea products, evidence of just how prevalent this problem can be in households where dogs reside.

The key to combating this parasite, two of which can become millions in a blink of an eye, is to launch your offense on three fronts: The dog, the house, and the yard. If you find one flea on your dog, which you are certainly likely to do on an active outdoor dog like the Malamute, then rest assured that your entire house and yard have been infiltrated not just by adult fleas, but by flea eggs and larvae as well. All must be targeted. If you treat only the dog, you will find that there are plenty more fleas from the environment ready to take up residence where those you destroy on the dog once lived.

The dog: Begin with the dog, treating it with effective yet safe flea products, perhaps a combination of bath, dip, and spray (all of which must be compatible with each other to prevent a toxic reaction; consult your dog's veterinarian for advice on mixing and matching).

The home: While the dog is being treated, attack the household as well. A variety of sprays and bombs are available that will destroy both adult and preadult (eggs and larvae) fleas that may be hiding in the carpet, the furniture, the dog's bed, your bed, virtually anywhere and everywhere.

The yard: Finally, give the same attention to the yard, for here too you will find fleas and their families just waiting to hitch a ride on the family dog for an entree into the house.

The warmer months of the year are typically the time when fleas are the greatest problem, so for most owners, this is a seasonal battle. In some areas where the weather remains balmy most of the time, it rages year round. Either way, success requires an owner who is willing to commit to the three-pronged attack on a routine basis—even if this requires weekly bathing, dipping, and spraying at the height of the season. You can't simply snap a flea collar on a dog at the beginning of the summer and leave it at that. You must proceed with the correct ammunition, and use all flea products only as directed.

Although the nuts and bolts of flea control have not changed much in recent years, researchers are always looking for that magic bullet that will render flea control obsolete. This has led to some promising new advancements in flea control, such as a new oral remedy that prevents preadult fleas from maturing, as well as topical products applied directly to the dog. Regardless of the type of flea control program you pursue, it's always wise to discuss it first with your dog's veterinarian, as he or she will be best able to advise you on what will be the safest and most effective route for your particular dog.

Ticks

When you declare war on fleas, as an added bonus you will probably be targeting ticks, as well, for the products that destroy the former usually do the same to the latter. While ticks are not a threat to every dog, because of the diseases they carry, such as Lyme disease, they can be a serious prob-

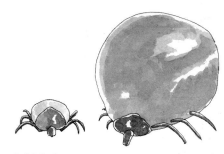

A tick before and after a meal.

lem for dogs that spend a great deal of time outdoors in tick country, which Malamutes often do.

Flea control products applied as directed to the dog before it ventures into the wilderness home of ticks should help keep the parasites at bay, but check your dog's skin carefully from head to toe after you leave tick country just to be sure.

If you should find a tick on your dog's skin, you cannot simply brush it away as you would a fly. Grasp the round body of the tick and as much of its head as possible firmly between your thumb and forefinger, and pull it out slowly with a sure, steady movement. Apply a topical antibiotic ointment to the site to prevent infection, and watch the dog for several weeks to make sure it does not begin to exhibit signs of illness, stiffness, or lethargy that could be related to a tick-borne illness.

The Picture of Health

The Veterinary Partnership

Nothing, absolutely nothing, is more stunning, more breathtaking, than the beautifully turned-out Alaskan Malamute with a clean, lustrous double coat, clear, alert eyes, a well-muscled physique, and an aura of stamina molded by centuries of existence in some of the most frigid regions of the globe. But while this vision of canine beauty is indeed the Malamute's legacy, it is not achieved without some effort on the part of that dog's owner, a responsibility every owner accepts as soon as he or she decides that this noble dog will be joining the household.

While the fostering of the Malamute's health and well-being begins at home, its continued success relies on the partnership between the dog's owner and its veterinarian. The owner depends on the veterinarian to provide the dog with both routine preventive care and the treatments required for injuries and illness, and the veterinarian relies on the owner's vigilant observations and knowledge of the dog so that he or she can in turn offer the most effective treatment possible.

Selecting the ideal veterinarian, then, is a great responsibility. While this alone need not be overly daunting, what can be is the cost of proper veterinary care. However, this is an element of Malamute ownership that should be considered long before the animal ever joins the household, and one that cannot be ignored once the commitment to ownership is made.

Several avenues exist for choosing your dog's veterinarian. First, ask for recommendations from other dog owners, from your dog's breeder, or even from local animal shelter personnel, all of whom will be well acquainted with the veterinarians in your area and their individual philosophies toward their vocation.

One visit will usually give you a good indication as to whether you and your dog are compatible with a particular practitioner. Observe carefully how the doctor interacts with your dog. Does this veterinarian seem truly passionate about animals in the tradition of James Herriot, or is he or she simply going through the motions for a fee? You can usually determine this by how the veterinarian touches and speaks to your dog. Does your dog seem comfortable around this individual? Do you feel free to ask questions, which are then answered clearly and concisely?

Take this opportunity, too, to ask about specific concerns you might

There are few sights as breathtaking as the noble, dignified Alaskan Malamute.

have for the future care of your pet. For example, how are off-hours emergencies handled? Will the doctor refer you to specialists, such as an ophthalmologist or orthopedist, if necessary?

In making these all-important evaluations, remember you are not beholden to remain with a veterinarian simply because he or she has treated your dog once or twice or even for a year or two. If you are for any reason dissatisfied, keep looking. Your pet should enjoy many years of health and contentment, and through those years you want to work with a veterinarian who will not only see the dog through its many stages of life, but who will also make both you and your pet feel comfortable with every visit.

A Keen Eye

In addition to choosing a veterinarian, the most critical step toward optimum health care of an Alaskan Malamute—or of any dog—is preventive care. Nowhere is the partnership between owner and veterinarian more critical. Only if the owner takes seriously the responsibility of taking the dog to the veterinarian for those all-important routine checkups and vaccinations can the doctor provide the dog with the preventive care that will protect it year in and year out.

The same diligence must apply to the owner's care and observations of the dog at home. In virtually every potential health problem that can affect a beloved pet, from parvovirus to heartworm to cancer, early diagnosis is key to the dog's recovery and even survival. If you know your dog well when it is healthy, you will be better prepared to recognize immediately when things just aren't right.

Dogs cannot tell the doctor what is ailing them. Sometimes a veterinarian's ability even to determine where it hurts can be a challenge. But there are telltale signs that indicate that all is not

Though it presents a noble, dignified appearance, the twinkle in the Malamute's eye reveals the sense of fun that lurks within.

right with the animal, and the observant owner can recognize these signs quickly and easily, ideally in the earliest stages of an illness' progression.

Early Signs of Illness

The classic signs of illness in a dog can be fairly standard from illness to illness. Diarrhea, vomiting, and a loss of appetite, for example, are not illnesses in and of themselves, but rather *signs* of illness that obviously deviate from what is normal for the healthy dog. These three symptoms in particular can mean something as minor as a simple gastric upset, or something as critical as a case of parvovirus, and often only the veterinarian can determine the cause.

The sudden development of a limp that could indicate joint problems or the onset of hip dysplasia; the incessant shaking of the head, which is the classic sign of an ear infection or embedded foxtail; or even a dog's drastic

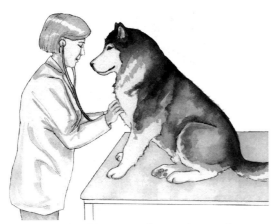

A solid program of preventive veterinary care, which includes annual checkups, can help a dog live well into its teens.

change in behavior, such as a typically gregarious dog's sudden swing into lethargy, are all signals that should send the owner to the phone for a call to the veterinarian. Malamutes tend to be linked quite closely to their owners and are usually more than willing to let them know as best they can that something just isn't right. It is then up to the dog's owner to heed those signals and act accordingly.

Even if the dog is showing no signs of illness or unusual behavior, keep your eyes open and make home examinations part of the daily, or at least weekly, care routine. Do some hands-on work, as well. During grooming, examine both coat and skin for changes in texture or landscape. Smell the ears for strange odors or a change in their normal scents. Take a look at the groin for lumps, bumps, or anything else that might be unusual there. Pay attention to the dog's frequency and ease of urination, and examine feces each day, as well. This will all better prepare you to recognize abnormal signs should they emerge later on—and you can guarantee that

something will at one time or another in the course of your pet's life.

Magic in a Syringe

Perhaps the most important players in the preventive medical care of the Alaskan Malamute are the dog's routine vaccinations. Thanks to relatively recent advancements in the veterinary care of companion animals, we now have access to a variety of vaccines that protect our pets from illnesses that at one time ran rampant and spelled certain death for the unfortunate animals that contracted them.

These vaccinations, which should begin during puppyhood, involve a series administered over several months' time. During its first weeks of life a puppy is protected by the maternal antibodies it receives from its mother's milk. After weaning, those antibodies can remain in the pup's system, rendering its vaccinations impotent. Thus only a series of vaccinations can help guarantee full protection in the long run.

The puppy should receive its first vaccination—a combination of infectious canine hepatitis, canine parvovirus, leptospirosis, canine coronavirus, and canine distemper—at six weeks of age. This should be repeated every three weeks thereafter until the puppy has received a series of four vaccinations and has reached 16 weeks of age. Recent research has further indicated that an extra parvo vaccination, perhaps at five or six months of age, is also beneficial. It seems the maternal immunity for that particular disease may remain within the puppy's system longer than it does for the other diseases. Once the initial vaccination series is complete, the dog should receive a booster every year thereafter to ensure its continued protection.

Not included in that combination vaccination is the rabies vaccination, which the puppy should receive at four months of age; in most areas this is required by law and a prerequisite for licensing. Depending on the particular vaccination the dog receives, it will require a rabies booster either every one or three years.

The rabies vaccination, which protects the dog from a disease that is 100 percent fatal, is critical for any dog, but of special concern for a dog as outdoorsy in nature as the Alaskan Malamute. This dog thrives best when afforded ample time in the great outdoors, where it may encounter a variety of rabies-prone animals, such as skunks and raccoons, that its predatory nature may lead it to chase, with dire results.

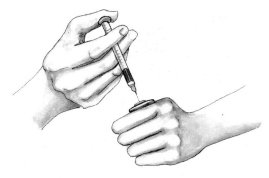

After its initial series of puppy vaccinations, the adult Malamute should receive annual boosters to protect it from a number of severe canine diseases.

The Case for Spaying and Neutering

One would not typically categorize a surgical procedure within the realm of preventive measures, but that is indeed where spaying and neutering belong. For many an owner, viewing the procedures in this light begins by overcoming the natural human inclination to cringe at the thought of the surgical removal of the sex organs. Cast that reflex aside, and you are looking at one of the kindest actions you can take as a dog owner, both for the health of the individual dog and for the species at large.

The results are in and they are indisputable. The altered dog, whether it is the spayed female or the neutered male, is generally healthier and longer lived than its intact counterpart, and it is likely to be a far superior pet. On the health front, the altered female, especially when she is spayed during puppyhood, is less prone to such maladies as mammary cancer and the various infections unique to the uterus and related organs. The same is true of the neutered male, which, after this very routine procedure, is far less likely to contract such illnesses as anal tumors and testicular cancer.

Spaying and neutering provide mental health benefits, as well. Malamute owners, for example, typically find that altering this particular breed can make so large an animal easier to handle. This is not to say that the procedures in any way diminish the dog's energy levels or make it any less of an athlete or exercise companion. Rather, the altered Malamute is less likely to roam, as such behavior is typically linked to a search for a mate, and it is more attuned to its owner than to the activities and scents of others of its own kind. Isn't that why we choose to live with dogs in the first place?

Nevertheless, despite the great benefits of spaying and neutering, which should override any emotional human responses, the myths persist. Altered dogs are fat, we hear. Altered dogs are lazy. Not so. Weight gain and lethargy are products of an owner's inattention to a dog's exercise needs and a propensity to overfeed, both of which have nothing to do with the animal's ability or inability to reproduce.

And finally, spaying and neutering bring the dual reward of being socially responsible, as well. With so many

67

dogs, including purebred Alaskan Malamutes, ending up in shelters and with rescue groups each year, ensuring that one's pet will never contribute to that problem is not only a smart choice to make on a personal level, but of great benefit to the dog population, as well.

Common Canine Ailments

Even with the most vigilant preventive care, illness is usually inevitable at one time or another during the long life of your beloved Alaskan Malamute. The following are a few conditions to watch for, and to act on as soon as any suspicious symptoms raise their ugly heads:

Canine Bloat

A profound veterinary emergency, canine bloat, also known as gastric dilitation-volvulus, occurs when a buildup of gas and/or fluid accumulates in a dog's stomach, which may then rotate, block off any chance of that buildup dissipating, and thus constrict the dog's circulatory system.

A dog suffering from bloat will exhibit signs of restlessness and abdominal pain; its stomach will swell, and it will salivate excessively and attempt unsuccessfully to vomit or defecate. As the condition progresses, and if the stomach twists, the dog will go into shock. Without immediate veterinary attention, which may include surgery to turn and anchor the stomach into the proper position, the dog can die.

As a member of the larger family of dogs, Malamutes are prone to canine bloat that, though it can affect any dog, typically targets larger animals as its victims. There are measures an owner can take to prevent it. Because its occurrence is directly linked to eating habits, Malamute owners should prevent their pets from gulping their food and from drinking large amounts of water after eating, habits common

in multidog households, in which dogs may believe they must eat quickly or lose their food to another dog. In such households, dogs should be fed separately and in individual dishes.

Of equal value is feeding pets several small meals throughout the day rather than one large meal, and preventing dogs from exercising vigorously right after eating. Following mealtime, it is wise as well to keep an eye on the dog, just to make sure it does not begin to exhibit signs of bloat that will require immediate treatment.

Heartworm Disease

A devastating illness transmitted by mosquitoes, heartworm disease is caused by a worm that settles in the dog's heart and, without treatment, ultimately kills its host. Treatment can be long and traumatic and prove almost as dangerous to the dog as does the infestation of the heartworms themselves.

Given the severity of this disease, not to mention of its treatment, it is worth your while to protect your pet from this devastating illness, and it is indeed fortunate that this can be done effectively with veterinary assistance. This begins with a blood test to determine that the dog is clear of infestation, followed by the administration once a month of a prescription preventive that will protect the dog from this devastating disease.

Heatstroke

If you leave your Malamute in the car during summer, allow it to over-exert itself in the heat, or confine it to an area of direct sun with no shade or water—especially this dog, which was born and bred for life in the frigid North—you are asking for trouble. Within minutes the temperature within that hot car, for instance, even with the windows down and parked in the shade, can climb to well above 100°F

(37.8°C), and the dog can succumb within an equally short period of time.

Dogs in general have a very low tolerance for heat, their only mechanism for cooling their bodies being the panting reflex, which is not all that effective. A dog afflicted with heatstroke will pant frantically, salivate profusely, perhaps stagger and vomit, and ultimately lapse into a coma that, without treatment, will lead to death. Treatment involves a gradual cooling of the animal with a bath or hose-down of cool (not cold) water, and a move to a cooler, shadier, preferably air-conditioned, environment.

The goal is to lower the animal's body temperature to 103°F (39°C), and many cases do require an emergency trip to the veterinarian to ensure that the condition is properly halted and reversed. Because such efforts are not always successful, a better alternative is to prevent the need for this in the first place by ensuring that the dog is never placed at risk in a hot car, subjected to direct sun for prolonged periods or time, enticed to participate in inappropriately hot exercise periods, or refused an ample supply of cool, clean water.

Hereditary Disorders

Like all pure breeds of dogs, the Alaskan Malamute is prone to several genetic problems. Most of these, however, can be avoided by purchasing a dog or puppy only from parents that have tested clear of the conditions, and by refusing to breed a dog that has such problems either itself or in its background.

Hip dysplasia is one such condition. While it may occur in various degrees of severity, hip dysplasia typically becomes apparent in a dog by the time it reaches its second birthday. The condition is a potentially crippling deformity of the hips that can affect any dog, but it is most prevalent in large dogs. As it progresses, the affected dog will exhibit increasingly dramatic signs of pain, move stiffly, perhaps limp, and even decline invitations to play and exercise. Treatment, depending on the severity of the condition, may range from pharmaceutical pain management to surgery. The incidence of hip dysplasia is tracked by the Orthopedic Foundation for Animals. Dogs that test clear after being x-rayed at two years of age are considered OFA certified and are the only animals that should be bred.

The OFA has also begun tracking *hypothyroidism,* which is on the increase in Malamutes. In this, the most common hormonal affliction of the canine species, a sluggish thyroid gland cannot secrete sufficient amounts of thyroid hormone. This in turn causes the dog to gain weight, grow uncharacteristically lethargic, and perhaps experience hair loss and related skin and coat problems. Once identified, the condition can usually be reversed with hormone replacement therapy, which the patient will probably require for the remainder of its life.

Chondrodysplasia (ChD), also known as dwarfism, is a heartbreaking hereditary condition, in which the affected dog is born with deformed legs that grow increasingly so as it matures. As a recessive condition, both parents must be carriers for their offspring to develop chondrodysplasia, but even a carrier dog that exhibits no signs should not be bred. To combat the problem, the Alaskan Malamute Club of America has established the Chondrodysplasia Certification Committee to identify affected dogs and carriers, and alert owners and breeders to the dogs that should not be bred. Only by honoring this program can breeders hope to eradicate the condition.

Internal Parasites

While most parasites will not prove deadly to an affected dog (unless that dog is quite young), their presence does undermine the dog's overall health and interferes with its optimum quality of life.

Internal parasites, such as the very common roundworms and tapeworms, which make their homes in the dog's intestines, can be easily discovered in the dog's feces, assuming, of course, that the owner is attuned to such necessary unpleasantries. The presence of tapeworms, for example, is easily detectable by the ricelike tapeworm segments that appear in the affected dog's feces or around its anus. As for roundworms, the owner should be willing to bring a fecal sample from his or her pet to the veterinarian twice a year for evaluation. In both cases, the worms can be easily eradicated upon diagnosis with prescription medications.

You can further prevent tapeworms, which are transmitted by fleas, by instituting a sound flea control program (see page 62). In the case of other various and sundry intestinal worms, preventing the dog from coming into contact with potentially infested feces of other dogs is the key to keeping your pet's insides parasite-free.

Kennel Cough

So named because it is most often transmitted from dog to dog in kennel situations, kennel cough, or canine infectious tracheobronchitis, is a highly contagious, though not typically serious, condition that affects a dog's respiratory system. One experience with kennel cough—particularly the harsh, honking, dry cough that can remain with the animal for a week or two or even longer—and it is understandable why owners would want to protect their pets, and themselves, from this ordeal.

Prevention of this illness is simple enough, provided by a vaccine known as *Bordetella,* that may be administered either by injection or through the nostrils. Any dog that is to be kenneled should receive this vaccine (and any self-respecting kennel will mandate that all canine residents be vaccinated), as well as dogs that will be experiencing dog-to-dog contact in show situations, sled dog races, weight pulls, at dog parks, or at field trials. When choosing a kennel, it is also wise to go with one that is kept squeaky clean, as cleanliness, too, is directly linked to the spread of kennel cough.

Parvovirus

A dog that develops diarrhea (especially diarrhea tinged with blood), that becomes lethargic, refuses to eat, and is feverish, may be suffering from canine parvovirus, a serious viral infection that affects the intestines. While the disease cannot be combated directly, immediate veterinary attention is imperative to provide the supportive fluid therapy required to enable the patient's own body to remain properly hydrated and fight off the infection. Hospitalization, therefore, is vital if this disease's victim is to survive, which can be touch and go depending on the dog's age and overall health before the illness strikes.

Although most dogs are protected from this disease by their annual vaccinations, it is not unusual for even a vaccinated dog to become infected. You might increase your pet's chances of avoiding parvovirus by keeping a puppy somewhat isolated from other dogs or areas that may be vectors of the disease until it has had its full series of vaccinations. Take care, too, to keep your pet's living quarters and kennel or similar areas it frequents clean and disinfected.

Skin Problems

A routine grooming program, as well as hands-on examinations of your pet from head to tail conducted on a weekly or more frequent basis, are the most effective ways to discover skin problems your dog may be developing. A variety of them exist, caused by everything from flea-bite allergies to bacterial infections to mange, and as is the case with most canine illness, early detection and diagnosis can help ensure that even stubborn skin problems can be conquered with ease.

Lumps, bumps, dryness, incessant scratching, hair loss, and redness are the classic signals that a dog is suffering from skin problems, most of which require a veterinarian's diagnosis to ensure proper treatment. While many conditions may indeed be a challenge to eradicate, some can be prevented through diligent care of the coat and skin (such as swift removal of the Malamute's undercoat when it begins to "blow" once or twice a year), and a sound flea control program.

Urinary Tract Disorders

Dogs are prone to a variety of diseases that can affect the urinary tract, most of them uncomfortable and painful to the dog, many of them quite serious.

Whether caused by a bladder infection, bladder stones, or kidney failure, any sign of urinary tract disease is reason to call the veterinarian. The most vivid signs of a problem here include a dog's painful or lack of urination, blood in the urine, a sudden increase in thirst and urination, or any change in urinary habits. Most are fairly evident to the observant owner.

Treatment, of course, depends on cause, which must be determined by a veterinarian who will use such tests as urinalysis and blood tests for diagnosis. Whether it involves medication, surgery or dietary management, treatment should begin as soon as possible to help prevent the condition from progressing to more dangerous, and possibly deadly, levels, and to relieve the dog's obvious discomfort.

In Case of Emergency

While early diagnosis is key to the successful treatment of any canine ailment, immediate recognition and fast action in some circumstances may be all that stand between survival and death for a dog in an emergency situation. Recognition of acute abdominal pain, for one, should tell an owner that immediate veterinary care is in order, as the cause may be something as critical as bloat or an intestinal obstruction.

Emergency care is most frequently associated with canine injury or similar external causes. An active Alaskan Malamute may be placed in situations where its vigorous lifestyle leads to injuries that may or may not be life threatening, but that in either case require emergency care. A bleeding wound, for example, may require treatment that can't wait for the veterinarian; in other words, this dog's survival may rely solely on an owner who knows to apply direct pressure to the wound with a clean cloth to stop the bleeding.

Indeed, life in the great outdoors can hold a variety of emergency threats to this active animal, including snakebite, broken bones, and shock, the latter of which is frequently the

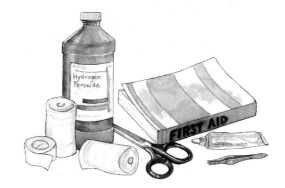

When embarking on an adventure with your Malamute, make sure to bring along a well-stocked first aid kit. You never know when you might be faced with an emergency.

result of some other primary catastrophe. Given the fact that many activities in which Malamutes participate are isolated from a neighborhood veterinarian, the owner should prepare ahead of time, both by assembling a well-stocked first aid kit (and making sure it is available both at home and away), and by learning how to use the items in it, as well as the various techniques of caring for a dog in specific emergency situations.

The first aid kit should contain the following:
• a large collection of bandages in various sizes
• adhesive tape in one-inch (25 mm) and two-inch (51 mm) widths
• cotton dressing pads
• rubber gloves
• antibiotic ointment
• cotton balls and cotton swabs
• prescription tranquilizer (some veterinarians recommend Benadryl as an emergency tranquilizer)
• saline eyedrops
• snakebite kit (available at most camping and large pet supply stores)

• diarrhea medicine
• hydrogen peroxide
• rubbing alcohol (which can also be used to remove tree sap from the coat)
• scissors
• clean towels
• tweezers
• petroleum jelly
• needle-nose pliers
• prescription painkiller
• activated charcoal tablets

Another key ingredient in the first aid kit should be a detailed canine first aid guide. While in-depth treatment details for most emergencies that might befall the active Malamute extend beyond the scope of this book, completing your canine first aid kit with a book dedicated to that subject, and familiarizing yourself with its contents long before you must act to help your dog, will ensure your pet has the best chance of survival should an emergency occur.

If your dog seems a likely candidate for first aid measures because of the lifestyle it shares with you, why not practice ahead of time, too? Learn to apply splints, learn to treat for shock by keeping the dog still and warm, and even learn how to treat snakebite. Your dog will probably view such exercises as a game, but in the long run, that game could save the animal's life.

Poisoning, too, requires fast action; therefore, the savvy owner will remain attuned to the signs of poisoning and, in turn, what potential poisons the dog may have ingested in its environment (such as antifreeze, poisonous plants, or even chocolate). Beyond these obvious measures, be sure to keep the local poison control number on hand, as well. Treatment for some poisons require vomiting, for example, while others absolutely do not, and the poison control personnel are the best resources for determining how to combat each type.

Attention to the Alaskan Malamute's overall health throughout its life will help to make its older years rewarding, comfortable, and a very special time for both the dog and its family.

Care of an Old Friend

Care for a dog with diligence and love, and the dog will reap the benefits of living a long and healthy life. Indeed one of the most delightful stages of the dog's life comes in its older years, when physically it may slow down a bit, but emotionally it enters a phase when the bond between dog and owner takes on a special glow.

With proper care throughout its life, there is no reason that the Alaskan Malamute cannot enjoy a rewarding and active quality of life well into its teens. This is not to say that things won't change a bit. The Malamute that once spent every weekend showing off its skills in agility, leading a dog team through the snow, or jogging five miles (8.1 km) with an owner in triathlon training may have to modify its activities a bit as it ages. Still, exercise must remain paramount in this dog's schedule, for both the dog's and the owner's well-being.

Walks: One of the most productive commitments you can make toward the care of the older dog is to make room each day for a nice, long walk. Daily walks help keep the older dog's (and the younger dog's) mind clear, its aging joints lubricated, its digestive tract stimulated, and its muscles toned. It also helps keep the dog's weight in check, as many older dogs suffer from an increase in pounds that only serves to stress its aging body and internal systems.

Examinations: The veterinarian plays a key role in the care of the older dog, as well. Geriatric exams conducted twice a year, in which the veterinarian checks the dog's urine and blood, can help detect any budding health problems at the earliest opportunity, and see that treatment begins before those problems have a chance to get worse. The doctor may also recommend adjusting the dog's diet to one of fewer calories and less fat, or to one of the prescription diets now available to help control any health problems the animal may be developing related to aging.

Seeing and hearing problems: Other potential changes require even more of an owner's commitment. As it ages, for example, the dog's sight or hearing may diminish, but this in no way need detract from the animal's quality of life. Dogs tend to adjust well to these natural changes, assuming that their owners meet the new challenges with patience and understanding. Refrain from moving the furniture around at this time if your dog is losing its sight, and prepare for the possibility of a dog losing its hearing by teaching it both verbal commands and hand signals during those formative training years. That way you can be assured of communicating with each other throughout the dog's life.

All in all, there are few callings more rewarding than caring for the older dog. Building a strong foundation of health and mutual respect that will ensure a happy life later on is the first step, after which you will experience a special bond as the beloved companion upon whom you have always depended begins to depend more on you. It is a bond even more acute when shared with the Malamute, a dog that at any age exhibits a most legendary devotion to the human species and a special sensitivity to its family pack.

When It's Time to Say Good-bye

One of the saddest inevitabilities with which every devoted dog owner is intimately acquainted, is the fact that we are doomed to outlive our canine companions. Hand in hand with this fact comes the difficult challenge not only of saying good-bye, but of having to make the fateful decision of determining just when that time will be.

Although advancements in veterinary medicine have enabled dogs to live longer, more productive lives than ever before, the time inevitably comes when the dog is either too ill or too much in pain to go on. Although making such a decision can be incredibly devastating for the owner, it takes a great deal of courage and compassion to end that animal's suffering. The decision made, the veterinarian can humanely end the dog's life with an injection that simply puts the dog into a deep and peaceful slumber from which it will not awaken.

Whether the dog passes on naturally in its sleep, is euthanized humanely at the end of a long and productive life, or meets a more untimely, unexpected end, the grief of the owner left behind is genuine and something about which he or she should not be ashamed. Yes, there are individuals who scoff at such deep emotions for companion animals, but they are increasingly in the minority and are certainly missing out on one of life's greatest rewards. Dogs are in every sense family members, and it is perfectly legitimate, and even necessary, to grieve for their loss, whether alone, with trusted friends and family members, or even with one of the support groups that specialize in this particular type of grief.

While one's initial response to the loss of a longtime canine companion may be the thought that he or she will never have another dog, those who have been through it know that the enrichment these animals bring to our lives far outweighs any grief that inevitably comes at the end of the relationship. Which brings us to the question of welcoming another dog into the family.

Once a person has lived with an Alaskan Malamute, he or she often finds it quite difficult to live without one. The question is when to bring a new Malamute into the family. For some, the best remedy for healing the broken heart caused by the loss of one dog is to bring another into the home as soon as possible. For others, a period of mourning must occur before making the commitment again. Either way, when that new dog joins the family, you must not expect the new addition to be a clone of the first. Each is an individual with its own special brand of Malamute joy to bring to your home. Love and cherish this dog for who it is, just as you loved and cherished its predecessor.

The Breeding Question

To Breed or Not to Breed

We have explored in depth the great responsibility of caring for the Alaskan Malamute, but when we take so grand a dog as this into our home, a dog of the Arctic whose caretakers somehow preserved its appearance, athletic abilities, and heart for thousands of years despite unspeakable hardships, we see how this responsibility applies not only to the care of a single pet, but to the preservation of the breed at large.

When viewing the breed in this context, it is difficult to imagine someone taking the breeding of Malamutes lightly. Too often this happens with canine reproduction, however, much to the detriment of the breed in question. In the Malamute's case, this has led to the development of such genetic problems as hip dysplasia, night blindness, dwarfism, and hypothyroidism.

Considering the serious repercussions of casual breeding, one should not breed a dog based on misguided notions that there are abundant profits to be made from doing so. Stud fees, prenatal veterinary visits, plus the proper everyday care of the new mom and her puppies will quickly eat up any profits one imagines are inherent in this endeavor.

Nor should a parental desire for a child to experience "the miracle of life" be the motivation. Not only is this unfair to the puppies, but it neglects the fact that much can go wrong in the whelping of puppies, especially when it is done casually, and you could end up with a litter of orphaned pups who require 24-hour care if they are to survive.

In addition, the well-meaning family that seeks to breed their dog as a biology lesson, or because they believe their darling pet should have "just one litter" before she is spayed, too often end up giving the resulting puppies away to unsuitable homes out of desperation, or turning them over to the local animal shelter when they discover there really aren't enough homes out there after all—especially homes for dogs that could soon weigh 100 pounds (45.4 kg). This is not generally the message parents seek to impart to their kids about the responsibilities of pet care. A more positive lesson would be to explain to the kids why they won't be breeding their beloved pet, one reason being the fact that the altered pet is also usually a longer-lived pet.

There are legitimate reasons to breed a dog, too, of course, but these require a bit of soul searching.

The Ethical Breeder

The ethical, responsible breeder is an individual whose sole motivation for breeding a dog is to preserve the breed and to strive for that elusive standard of perfection. This means choosing breeding stock with utmost care for conformation, genetic background, and temperament, and adhering to the Alaskan Malamute Club's Code of Ethics, which means the breeder will be responsible for the puppies he or she breeds for the duration of the dogs' lives. It means doing everything possible to ensure that dogs affected by the breed's hereditary problems, no matter how beautiful, no matter how sweet tempered, remain out of the breeding program. It means choosing puppy buyers with great care and

Because of its wolflike appearance, the Alaskan Malamute, unfortunately, is the breed most commonly crossed with wolves for the breeding of wolf hybrids. This practice is, however, a violation of the Alaskan Malamute Club of America's Code of Ethics.

selling the pups with spay/neuter contracts and stipulations that the dogs be returned to the breeder should their owners need to relinquish them at any time in the future.

Responsible breeding means making whatever investments necessary of both time and money to ensure that the dam and her puppies receive the best care possible for their own benefit and for that of the Malamute family at large. This is an expensive proposition and an awesome responsibility, but when done with the purest motives, it is a labor of true love.

Wolf/Dog Hybrids: A Special Problem

While every breed of dog faces the pitfalls of irresponsible breeding, it presents a special problem to the world of Alaskan Malamutes: the problem of wolf/dog hybrids.

Just as Malamutes are frequently mistaken for wolves, so have they emerged as the ideal cross in misguided attempts to create a wolf with the temperament of a dog, but of course, genetics don't work that way. With few exceptions, the resulting offspring of such crossings tend to be unstable, usually mistreated animals, that in most cases end up with status-seeking individuals who have no business living with an animal of wolf breeding, let alone a domestic dog.

Wolf/dog hybrids tend to be large, powerful animals with a special affinity for destroying furniture, landscaping, and architecture, and far too many children have fallen victim to the animals' predatory reflexes. Most are virtually untrainable and cannot be housebroken. They are confused animals of both wild and domestic blood, thus their temperaments may never be considered completely reliable. With few exceptions, wolf/dog hybrids are inappropriate pets for the vast majority of the human population.

Once those misguided individuals who take these animals as pets recognize their grave error—realizing that no, this animal cannot reside in a two-bedroom urban condominium or be allowed anywhere near the family's four-year-old child—it is too late. The animal ends up the victim, perhaps beaten and/or imprisoned by the owner, abandoned on a country road or busy highway, or, if fortunate, relegated to one of the nation's over-crowded animal shelters. In most cases in which owners must be rid of a hybrid, the most humane answer is usually euthanasia. It is doubtful that most could ever be rehabilitated, and only a few individuals exist who know how to care properly for these animals in the first place. Also, recent court decisions in cases where children were attacked by hybrids adopted from shelters have held the shelters liable, thereby sending the message to shelters and individual breeders and owners alike, that perhaps it is not financially wise to adopt these animals out to the unsuspecting public.

So prevalent did the problem of wolf/dog hybrids become in the early 1990s, that communities across the nation began to ban the ownership of the animals, a trend that continues and is now doing great harm to the Malamute. Forbidden to keep hybrids, owners simply license them as Malamutes. Most people don't know the difference, and to date there is no DNA test that will offer conclusive identification. When the animals bite, as many do, thanks to their genetic instabilities and improper care, the bites are attributed to Malamutes, causing statistics for this breed to inflate unjustly. Many longtime Malamute enthusiasts, especially those involved with Malamute rescue, fear that ultimately this situation could lead to the undoing of their breed, first in labeling it a biting breed that may then be banned in some areas, and then in damaging its bloodlines by crossing it with an animal that is not even of its own species.

The bottom line then is this: When considering whether to breed your Malamute, do not even entertain the notion of crossing it with a wolf or of allowing others to do so for any price. You may come across some shady types with promises of large puppy profits, but they neglect to mention that most people who buy wolf/dog hybrids abandon the dogs before they reach two years of age, or that liability judgments against owners whose wolf/dog hybrids attack children (the most common victims) can reach into the hundreds of thousands of dollars.

If you do intend to breed your Malamute, to paraphrase a lyric from

The well-bred Malamute comes from parents that have been certified free of such genetic disorders as hip dysplasia, chondrodysplasia (dwarfism), and hypothyroidism.

the musical *West Side Story,* stick to their own kind. You will thus do the dog's progeny a great favor, and at the same time pay tribute to the heritage of all the Malamutes that have come before. The Malamute as a breed, as well as the puppies you produce, do not deserve to be merely the products of a fad or the means to getting rich quick.

The Mating Game

Obviously, the first step in dog breeding is to determine if your female dog is up to the task: She must be deemed free of genetic anomalies, especially evident if she is the offspring of parents declared free of chondrodysplasia (dwarfism) by the Alaskan Malamute Club of America, and both she and her parents must be certified clear of hip dysplasia by the Orthopedic Foundation for Animals. She should exhibit no sign of night blindness, nor should she be affected by the newest problem to affect her breed: hypothyroidism. Her temperament should be exemplary, and though

77

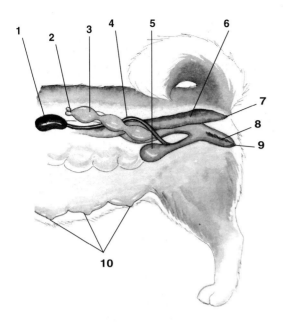

An internal view of the pregnant female:
1. kidney 2. ovaries 3. developing embryo
4. ureter 5. bladder 6. rectum 7. anus
8. vagina 9. vulva 10. mammary glands

there is no such dog as one that satis-
fies its breed standard perfectly, her
conformational faults should be minor.

Now use the same criteria in choosing your bitch's mate. He and his parents, also, should be certified free of
Malamute genetic problems. He, too,
should exhibit all the finest traits of
the Malamute, and his faults should
be offset by his potential mate and
vice versa.

The bitch's first prenatal veterinary
visit should take place before she
even meets her new mate. Have her
vaccinated and treated for any internal
parasites that may be lurking within.
This helps prepare her physically to
produce the healthiest puppies possible, and to ensure that her immunity,
which she will pass on to her puppies
through her milk, is freshly bolstered.

If you are new to this game, work
with your dog's breeder and veterinarian. The breeder probably knew from
the beginning that it was your goal to
breed and ideally helped you choose
an appropriate puppy for that (pet-
quality puppies, remember, should
receive limited registration from the
breeder and be altered according to
a spay/neuter contract). The breeder
probably also has some idea of who
would be an appropriate mate. The
veterinarian can contribute advice on
the mechanics and timing of mating.
Get to know the doctor well, because
you'll be seeing a lot of each other in
the weeks to come.

Once you have worked out the
logistics governing the mating of your
happy little couple, watch for the signs
of estrus. When your bitch goes into
heat (do not breed her during her first
or even second heat; wait for her to
mature), you will know the time is
right when she seems receptive to the
stud dog. After a few tussles, she will
allow him to mount her, a behavior he
learned as a puppy playing with his
littermates. It's best to monitor the
mating to be sure that neither dog
becomes aggressive or picks a fight;
someone could get hurt.

When the male dog enters the
female, his penis will become erect,
resulting in what is known as the tie.
He will essentially be held in by the
swelling, allowing the semen to flow
into the female. The tie can last anywhere from 5 to 60 minutes, during
which time the male dog may turn
around to face away from the female,
leaving the two standing end to end.
You may want to encourage the dogs
to repeat this little dance daily until the
bitch is no longer receptive to her
suitor's attentions.

Caring for the Mother-to-Be

At this point, the mating game now
becomes the waiting game. Your

safest bet is to assume your bitch is pregnant immediately and care for her accordingly. The most critical organ development of the puppies occurs during those first few weeks before their mother even begins to exhibit signs of pregnancy.

An experienced breeder can usually tell if a bitch is pregnant several weeks after the dog has been mated (although dogs have been known to exhibit all the signs of pregnancy without, in fact, being pregnant). Newcomers and experts alike, however, are usually most comfortable relying on the veterinarian's expertise in this department, not simply to diagnose pregnancy, but to assist in the entire process leading to the delivery of a healthy litter of puppies.

The new mother should be able to deliver her puppies herself, but sometimes she may require a bit of human assistance as the puppies come through the birth canal.

Diet

Given the personality, breeding history, and activity levels of your dog, the veterinarian can help you determine what is best for her during the weeks to come. Most canine moms-to-be will thrive on moderate exercise and a healthy commercial dog food, the rations of which will increase gradually at about the third week of pregnancy. By the end of her pregnancy, the bitch, depending on her individual metabolism and activity, should be receiving a 25 to 50 percent increase in her normal rations.

Because of the puppies' pressure on her internal organs, feed the expectant Malamute mom three or four small meals a day rather than one or two larger meals, and resist the temptation to ply her with treats. Stick to a healthy, well-balanced commercial diet that provides her with everything she needs, and you'll avoid obesity, which can hinder whelping. All in all, the bitch should experience an approximate 35 percent weight gain.

Preparation for Whelping

Alaskan Malamutes tend to be easy whelpers, but problems can always arise. Discuss the possibilities with the veterinarian, but also get some details on just what to expect and how the practitioner likes to handle whelping. For example, your veterinarian may prefer that the mother dog do most of the work herself, cutting the cords, ingesting the placentas, etc., and that you just stand by in case of an emergency.

On the other hand, the veterinarian may prefer that you be more actively involved in the delivery, helping to pull out the puppies, cleaning them, cutting their umbilical cords, etc. In either case, the doctor should instruct you in these procedures, and alert you to the danger signs you should look for that indicate veterinary intervention. Make sure, too, that either your veterinarian or an emergency practitioner will be available when the time comes.

The length of canine gestation can vary, but 63 to 65 days is fairly average. Sometime between the 30th and 40th day, your dog may begin to show signs of discomfort. She will gain most of her excess weight at the end of her pregnancy, and she won't be able to move around as gracefully as she once could.

As the big event grows imminent, she will grow restless and may pant heavily. She may follow you around like a shadow or succumb to an uncharacteristic desire to be alone. She may attempt to nest, an inkling you should accommodate by setting up her whelping box in a warm, dry, secluded area of the house.

The Whelping Box

The whelping box may be made of wood, plastic, or cardboard. Its sides should be low enough for the new mom to walk over, but high enough to keep the puppies inside. For bedding, use soft, clean towels that can be easily washed and changed; avoid newspaper, that, though convenient, can discolor the resident pups and even prove toxic to them. You may want to place a heating pad, covered with blankets and towels to prevent overheating, at one end of the box, providing a heat source to which the puppies can gravitate if chilled, and move away from if hot.

Help the mother-to-be get acquainted with the whelping box before she needs it. Gather the necessary supplies ahead of time, too. These should include:
• a bulb syringe (should you have to clear a puppy's airway of mucus or birthing fluids)
• antibiotic ointment
• scissors
• Betadine disinfectant
• thread or dental floss (to tie the umbilical cord)
• a flashlight
• cotton balls
• mountains of clean towels and blankets.

Keep the area very clean, warm, and secluded. It doesn't take much to stress a new mom either during or after delivery.

The Big Event

When it's time for whelping, settle the bitch into the whelping box and stand by. Before you know it, you should be seeing a wet sac containing a tiny puppy or the wet puppy itself coming through the birth canal. If you will be assisting in the delivery, wash your hands with antibacterial soap. With a clean washcloth lining your hand to prevent slippage, grasp the newborn's tiny form firmly by the head and shoulders and gently ease it into the world. Be warned, however, that the new mother may not appreciate your intervention.

Mom should begin licking the little package to clean off the birthing residue and to stimulate its breathing and circulation (if she needs help in doing this, rub the puppy's tiny body with a clean washcloth). She should also try to stimulate the pup's first urination and defecation (again, if you need to assist in this, rub the areas gently with a clean cotton ball dipped in warm water). If Mom neglects to do so, you may also need to cut the umbilical cord. With the thread or dental floss you gathered for just such an emergency, tie one knot in the cord about an inch (25 mm) from the puppy and another about a quarter of an inch (6.4 mm) up from that toward its mom. Make a clean cut between the two knots with your scissors and dip the exposed end attached to the puppy in Betadine.

The placenta: In the midst of all this, watch for the delivery of the placenta, which may come with the puppy or follow it. If left to her own maternal devices, the mother may eat the placenta. While some see this as beneficial, most experts believe the practice should be prevented, or that the new mother should be allowed to eat only one or two. Regardless of one's position on the subject, what is important is that you count the placentas carefully to be sure that the number of placentas delivered matches the number of puppies delivered.

Nursing: You may also need to help the puppy locate a nipple for that first all-important nursing from which it receives the antibody-rich colostrum. Its mother may allow this while she is delivering other puppies, or she may prefer to wait until all are accounted for. Your primary concern at this point should be that each new arrival remain warm and dry (use fresh towels and washcloths when handling each successive puppy), and watch closely for signs of distress in their mother, such as nonproductive contractions and pushing, a sudden end of labor, or outright cries of pain. If at all uncertain, call the veterinarian immediately. That is what he or she is there for.

Within 12 to 24 hours, the new little family should be settled in to the now well-populated whelping box. The bedding has been changed to provide a cozy, clean, dry nest. The room is warm, dim, and quiet, and the pups are happily suckling from their rather exhausted, though now much more comfortable, mother. Even with so idyllic a scene, within those first 24 hours, you should arrange for a postnatal veterinary check of both Mom and her puppies to make sure all are well. The veterinarian can inspect the pups for such subtle problems as cleft palates or low birth weights, and the new mother should be examined to make sure her milk is good, there are no retained placentas, no infections, and no hemorrhaging.

Proper Puppy Care

Once the puppies have arrived safely and soundly, if the new mother seems to be dedicated to her maternal duties, allow nature to take its course. Leave her alone to do her job; the care she offers her puppies and the canine social example she sets for them within the next few weeks can affect their behavior and temperament for the rest of their lives. But do watch

Mom and her puppies should be supplied with a clean, dry whelping box situated in a warm, quiet, private area of the house.

for potential health problems, change the bedding regularly, make sure Mom continues to eat as well as she did during her last stages of pregnancy to fuel her lactation demands, keep visitors to a minimum, handle puppies only when necessary and only with clean hands, and watch for signs that particular pups may not be thriving.

Your most effective barometers of puppy health are weight gain and body temperature. Healthy puppies, even when only a few days old, are round, plump, and robust, and they seem to put on weight every day. Blind and deaf, they wiggle when picked up and have a tendency to pile on top of each other for warmth. They exhibit lusty sucking reflexes even if what is presented for them to suck is a human finger. If they cry, they typically do so only because they are hungry, cold, or in pain, all of which you or their mother should be able to remedy.

The sick pup: If you notice a "lone wolf" among the pack—a puppy that doesn't snuggle in with its brothers and sisters, that seems to have difficulty suckling, that becomes easily chilled, and, most importantly, isn't gaining weight—that puppy may not survive. While this should be an isolated situation, if it seems that several or all of the puppies are failing to put on weight sufficiently, Mom may not be keeping up with their milk demands and you may have to help her out with some supplemental bottles of milk substitute.

Mother's milk: This is truly a nectar for canine health, not simply because it fosters the puppies' development, but also because it protects them immunologically. From their mother's milk the puppies receive maternal antibodies (hence the reason for having her vaccinated before she is impregnated), which will protect them until they begin receiving their own vaccinations at six weeks of age. Because of this, it's a good idea to keep the puppies indoors during their first formative weeks, even after they become more mobile and anxious to venture into new territory. If they happen to stumble across feces that contain parvovirus in a park, for example, the results can be deadly for the relatively unprotected pups.

As they grow: Within about 10 to 15 days these helpless little predators will begin to open their eyes and find a whole new world awaiting them. Each day they will make giant leaps in development: learning new games, interacting with siblings, exploring the fascinating sights, scents, and sensations that exist beyond Mom's lovely warmth. Resembling little bear cubs, their ears not yet erect, their snouts not yet elongated, the puppies will tumble, pounce, and probably chew on each other whenever the opportunity to do so arises.

Offer the puppies safe toys and make sure they stay away from such dangers as a poisonous poinsettia plant and electrical cords. Watch them with delight, but remind yourself constantly, just as you must remind would-be buyers, that soon those adorable little bun-

dles could weigh in excess of 80, 90, even 100 pounds (36, 41, 45.4 kg).

Weaning: The early stages of weaning will begin at about three or four weeks of age, at which time you may begin to introduce the puppies to a milky gruel served up in a low-sided stainless steel dish. This can be made up of evaporated milk, baby cereal, eggs, and/or whatever your veterinarian suggests. Soon thereafter you may introduce the pups to their first dry puppy kibble, but moisten it liberally with water to make it into a mush that is easy for them to eat. Little by little, you can reduce the moisture as the pups begin to nurse less and eat more solid food. By eight weeks of age, they should be fully weaned, they have received their first vaccinations, and they have been offered ample time to enjoy and learn from their mother's attentions, which all translates to a successful transition into a new human family.

Proper Placement of Pups

The greatest gift you can offer to the puppies you breed are good and permanent homes. That's all part of the deal. Locating just the right owners for six, eight, perhaps ten puppies can be an overwhelming challenge, especially in this day and age when people are constantly moving, divorcing, suffering financial hardship—all transitional problems that do not tend to bode well for family pets.

Yet, despite that challenge, you cannot lower your standards on what is deemed a decent home for the Malamute. It deserves someone who fits the Malamute owner standard to a T. Period. You must therefore do a tremendous amount of screening of prospective buyers to make sure that you are entrusting the fruits of your and the puppies' mother's labors to worthy souls. This involves extensive interviews, a visit to the prospective owner's home, and that all-important contract.

Your contract, like any reputable breeder contract, must address spaying and neutering, proper care, housing, genetic conditions, and, of course, the fact that the owner must return the dog to you at any time in the future for any reason if he or she can no longer keep it. This latter point is a clause you committed to the day you decided to breed your dog.

Tough goals to meet, you say? How will you ever find owners who will fill that substantial bill? People who tell you placing puppies is simple are probably not placing them carefully and are probably washing their hands of the pups once they are out of sight. Indeed, as you struggle with placement, there will be times you wish you could simply give them away "free to a good home" and be done with it, but you must not even consider such an option.

Aside from the fact that casual, even "free," placement forsakes all the necessary screening and contractual agreements from both parties, most people don't value what they receive for free and are therefore far more liable to treat it with apathy, cruelty, or even disdain—especially when the novelty of puppyhood wears off. It is then both the dog and its breed who suffer from an unprepared impulse on the part of

If you breed Malamutes according to the Malamute club's Code of Ethics, you are responsible for the puppies you produce for the rest of their lives.

the buyer, and a failure on the part of the breeder to uphold his or her end of the unspoken breeding contract with the Malamute breed.

So what happens if you can't locate the right homes? Well, look at the bright side. Given the fact that you are responsible for the fate of this litter anyway, you may just end up with a whole Malamute family permanently. As they say, when you get lemons make lemonade, so when you get six Malamute puppies, make a dog team!

A Commitment to Activity

Body and Soul

Bringing an Alaskan Malamute into your home means providing that dog with daily activity through which it may expend its abundant energies. No, you need not harness the dog to a sled for a rollicking jaunt through the snow—although your pet will be most pleased if you do so—but it must be entertained with plenty of exercise that will do you both good.

Exercise for a Malamute—or for any dog—does far more than simply work the dog's muscles, bones, and joints. The benefits of a solid exercise regimen are limitless in scope.

Yes, physical activity does keep a dog fit and probably living longer than it would if it were relegated to life as a couch potato. Yes, it helps prevent

The Alaskan Malamute is a large dog that requires an owner who is equally dedicated to activity in the great outdoors.

obesity, a condition epidemic in America's canine population today, and yes, it improves a dog's circulation and digestion. But an added bonus that many owners may not think of is the fact that when a dog gets out into the world, its mind as well as its body is stimulated by the experience, and the dog will end up being a better pet.

A dog that is accustomed to daily activity and interaction with the wonderful scents, sights, and sensations beyond the boundaries of its home turf is far less likely to become a victim of separation anxiety and a practitioner of home demolition and incessant barking. The dog is fulfilled body and soul and therefore has no reason to protest.

Do not think, however, that simply turning this dog out into your backyard will garner such benefits. There is no lazy way out of living with a Malamute. This is a partnership to which both partners must commit. That commitment is second nature to the Malamute, evident in the leaps of joy you will encounter every time the dog spots the leash in your hand, even if torrents of rain are falling outside or the weather report just informed you that it's 20-below with the wind chill.

Needless to say, the commitment may not come so easily to the human partner, who may at times be tempted to forget that the Malamute's high activity level was a characteristic that drew him or her to this breed in the first place. One way to deal with this is not to dread the time you must devote each day to acting as your Malamute's personal trainer, but to see it as natural to your day as eating or breathing. Your dog will certainly view it this way. Join it in its wisdom.

Health Considerations

Ideally, your Malamute should have its first introductions to physical activity as a young puppy. Its exuberant puppy antics, attacking tennis shoes, rolling under the coffee table, speeding through the halls after the kids, and puppy kindergarten fun, combined with restful naps and quiet times, will usher the youngster in to what awaits it as an adult. But, though the Malamute is a natural athlete of legendary strength and endurance, you must not ignore common sense in preparing it for physical activity. Consider the demands such activities will place on the dog, and prepare the animal accordingly.

If the dog has been relatively sedentary of late, perhaps receiving two half-hour walks a day, but you would like to venture into recreational mushing, ski-joring, agility, or even jogging with your dog, it must be introduced to the new vocation gradually so as not to overly tax its system or strain muscles. This will also give you time to introduce your pet to any special equipment that may be required, such as a harness or a different type of lead. Most Malamutes, excited by the prospect of a new adventure and driven by their compulsion to work with and please their owners, won't hold back when asked to work, regardless of their physical condition, so it's the owners' job to ensure they proceed safely.

The best bet is first to have the dog examined by the veterinarian to ensure it is up to the new tasks. The doctor can inspect the dog's legs, heart, lungs, and feet, and together you can discuss its diet as well as design a safe conditioning program. For jogging, this may simply mean keeping the dog on its usual mainte-

Ever ready for fun, the Alaskan Malamute must be provided with some sort of physical activity each and every day.

nance diet, enticing it to drink a bit more water, and starting it out running short distances that gradually lengthen every few days. For a newcomer to mushing, however, the doctor may prescribe a high-energy diet or nutritional supplements, as well as training exercises, in which the dog first pulls a wheeled cart along a clean, snow-free road before tackling winter conditions.

You must also consider the climate. For obvious reasons, most Malamutes work best in cooler, preferably cold, temperatures. It's the heat you need to worry about. During summer, therefore, restrict vigorous activity to the cooler times of the morning and evening. Make sure the dog is not exposed to direct sunlight or its feet subjected to hot pavement, and watch it carefully for heavy or shallow breathing, pale gums, profuse salivation, or a wobbly gait that could indicate heatstroke. And regardless of the weather, hot or cold, make

Given their history on the trail, Malamutes naturally take to backpacking with their owners and can easily carry their own supplies.

sure the dog drinks plenty of fresh, clean water throughout the day. You certainly don't want your efforts to satisfy your dog's energy needs to be tainted by unnecessary tragedy.

Activities within the Family

Although the Malamute will revel in the opportunity to work as a sled dog, this is not the only game in town for this breed. Malamutes excel in a variety of activities, most of which begin at home.

Daily walks: A family of committed Malamute owners can provide their pet with plenty of mental and physical stimulation without ever leaving the dog's hometown. While the suburban neighborhood may seem old hat to you, each day offers a whole new treasure trove of exciting, as-yet-to-be-discovered sights, smells, and experiences to the dog.

You can thrust your dog into the midst of this homespun adventure simply by taking it out on daily walks twice a day, preferably with the whole family in tow. Because the Malamute is a sled dog by breeding, it may be inclined to pull ahead. To remedy this,

some owners have come to prefer an H-shape harness or a head halter to the more traditional neck collars. Used correctly, the halter in particular, along with some training in this area, can help temper the dog's impulse to pull.

Regardless of what you choose in the way of walking equipment, relax. Unless you are seeking an obedience title, simply convincing the dog not to pull is more important (and more fun) than mastering the perfect heel. So go ahead and give the dog its head and stop occasionally to allow it to sniff and explore. After all, that's what you're here for, and you, too, could probably afford to stop from time to time and smell the proverbial roses.

Hiking: If you would like to carry walking a step further, try hiking with your pet, another natural occupation for this dog that is content to follow its owner anywhere—especially if there is snow on the ground. Begin with half-day hikes, and work up to the whole day once you're both up to it. So inspired, you may even want to try an overnight backpacking trip. A well-trained Malamute will gladly carry its own pack, which it may want to do on your shorter walks, as well.

Regardless of whether you are walking for half a day or a weekend, bring along ample supplies for the dog, including healthy treats and food, water, bedding, and a first aid kit. Remember, too, to abide by all rules: Pack out what you pack in (food leftovers, garbage, etc.), keep the dog on leash at all times, and don't allow the dog to harass wildlife. By obeying the rules of the trail, you will help ensure that the trails remain open to dogs in the future.

Hot wheels: Because of its size, talents, and conformation, the Malamute is somewhat grounded in what it can do in the way of exercise. You, on the other hand, are not. Yet even when you are participating in an activity that takes you above the ground on a set of wheels, your Malamute may still join you as an active and willing participant.

The most popular of such activities are bicycling and roller skating (either with in-line skates or the old fashioned four-wheel variety). Once you decide that you would like to teach your dog to lope alongside you as you ride a bike or skate, don't for a minute forget that the partner you are inviting along is a sled dog in mind and heart. In other words, it harbors an inner and almost uncontrollable desire to pull. If not properly trained to accompany a cyclist or skater, the results when its innate pulling instincts kick in can be devastating to the party on wheels at the other end of the leash.

Train the dog to join you in these pursuits in much the same way you teach it other skills. Make each experience as positive as it can be, which should be a breeze considering that the Malamute is a perfect candidate to accompany you on these forays.

Start with the fundamentals. Work first in perfecting your dog's skills on leash, perhaps with a halter or H-shape harness, convincing this big powerful dog that pulling on the leash really isn't what it should be doing. Work on this until you trust the dog implicitly not to pull while you are walking or running, then try it on wheels. Build up distances gradually, a benefit both to the dog's health and to helping the animal adjust to the new sensation of running alongside someone on skates or a bicycle.

Think of your own safety, too. Wear a helmet if you are cycling with a Malamute by your side; wear knee pads and elbow pads if you are bringing your dog along while you skate. You never know when a sudden impulse, scent, or sound will capture your pet's imagination and it shoots off in search of a wandering cat or in answer to a simple and sudden urge

Rollerblading provides a wonderful activity in which both owner and Malamute can participate, but proceed carefully with the proper equipment and the acknowledgment of just how powerful this large sled dog can be.

to run. Should this occur, you'll be thankful you took the time to outfit yourself with safety gear that can prevent the type of serious injuries that can only happen when one is on wheels and being pulled by a Malamute.

Snow and Cold: The Malamute's Calling

While a Malamute can enjoy any number of activities, its heart is where the snow is. Take an adult Malamute who has never seen snow up to the mountains in winter for an introduction. The blanket of white and the cold rustling through its coat will instantly trigger an ancient preprogrammed passion in the dog and summon those ancient memories. This is home. You may never convince the dog to leave.

The truly fortunate Malamute belongs to people whose motivation for obtaining such a dog was to spend time with it in the snow, whether or not they happen to live in snow country. Make the effort, and your Malamute will be eternally grateful.

An effective way to condition Malamutes for sledding work is to harness the dogs to a wheeled cart.

Mushing: The sport of mushing has enjoyed burgeoning popularity in the past few years. While such annual races as the Iditarod and the Yukon Quest attract more interest each year, and mushers lobby persistently to see sled dog racing become an Olympic sport, even those who aren't up to entering the legendary 1,000-plus-mile (1,610-plus-km) endurance races can enjoy this sport on a recreational basis.

The beauty of mushing with a Malamute is that, because this dog is a freighting dog rather than a classic racer, you only need one or two dogs to make a team. Participation does require some preparation, of course, both in training and in procuring the right equipment. You will need a sled, and you will need proper harnessing, which are available from specialty supply houses, both through mail order and from manufacturers typically located in regions where sledding is popular. Ideally, you will also need snow, but you can get by harnessing the dog to a

wheeled cart, which is actually a good way to condition and train the dog when there is no snow available.

Before you really get started, however, attend some mushing events and visit the mushers you meet there. The benefit of the sport's increasing popularity is that you are now more likely to find such events advertised in local newspapers. If not, contact your local kennel club as well as the national breed clubs for the sledding breeds. These sources should be able to point you in the right direction, and they may also be able to recommend trainers in your area, who instruct beginners on the sport of mushing.

Given that mushing is not the ideal sport for do-it-yourself training, learning hands-on from the experts is the smartest and safest way to go. Most newcomers are astounded at the terrific power that emanates from sled dogs as they revel in the role for which they were bred and born. That power can be dangerous in the hands of an untrained novice, so get the training you and your dog need, from handling the sled to the proper commands, and enjoy.

Skijoring: If you find the idea of mushing a dog team through the snow a bit too intimidating, there is an alternative: skijoring. In a more exciting, fast-action version of cross-country skiing, instead of a sled, you are on skis and the dog does what it loves most—it pulls you through the snow.

Although skijoring sounds simpler than classic mushing, it can be dangerous, so it is wise to get formal training, and while skijoring is more accessible to most people than mushing, it can also be more of a challenge as it is just you and the dog—no sled as a buffer.

To master the skill of skijoring, you should first master the art of standing up and getting around on skis; otherwise, the dog lurches forward, you fall over, and the rest becomes a very painful, very cold, very wet, memory. At the same time, work with the dog without skis, polishing up the obedience commands and mimicking skijoring by running with your dog (preferably in the snow). Expand your pet's vocabulary by working on turning and stopping commands, which will be vital out on the trail.

Soon you will be entrusting your well-being to the dog, so you must be able to trust this powerful animal, and to control it. For your first outing—preferably with your instructor—choose a relatively quiet, familiar, flat area, free of distractions and overly challenging trails. Build up the time you spend at it gradually, and remember not to skimp on the harnessing. Whether mushing a team of dogs from a sled or sharing a singular skijoring excursion with your beloved pet, proper harnessing can make the experience more pleasant—and safe—for you both.

For both sled work and skijoring, proper harnessing is a must for the safety of both dog and musher, or skijorer.

The Alaskan Malamute destined for the conformation show ring must learn to stand, or stack, correctly so it can be examined by the judge.

The winners of each group in a conformation dog show ultimately contend for coveted Best in Show honors.

The Show Spotlight

Formal showing is a unique avenue open to those who seek to get involved in what is known as the sport of dogs. In addition to providing a showcase for dogs, dog shows also offer a convenient opportunity for would-be Malamute owners to meet breeders and their dogs in a single location. Even if you choose not to show your dog, the shows can be paradise for those who revel in the company of purebreds.

Conformation Showing

Often referred to as beauty pageants for dogs, conformation shows, in which dogs are judged for appearance and movement as they are trotted around a ring by a handler, represent far more than simply a venue for owners to show off their pets. The purpose of the conformation show is to foster the breeding of dogs that meet their breed standards; the working breeds are judged on how well they embody the structure required for the jobs they have long been bred for.

Yes, the dogs in the conformation show ring are beautifully turned out,

well groomed, obedient, and attentive, but because the champion Malamute's legs and shoulders are of the correct angles, because its coat is of just the right texture and density, because its bite is perfectly aligned, and because its back is not too short or too long, this dog, theoretically, would also be ideally engineered for its work in the snow. Of course, it doesn't always happen that way—most show dogs never even participate in the vocations for which they were bred—but the theory is sound.

At AKC dog shows, registered Malamutes compete in the Working Group. The entrants are pitted first against other Malamutes, the winners ultimately making their way through several rungs until the Best of Breed is determined. The Best of Breed winner then competes against all the other Working Group Best of Breed winners for the Best of Group title. Within this competition the dogs are to be judged not against each other, but on how well each exemplifies its individual standard. Should the Malamute be chosen best of the Working Group, it then moves on to compete for the coveted title of Best in Show.

The ideal show dog is the dog who stands as a shining example of its standard, but who also truly enjoys prancing around that ring. In addition to physique and movement, judges look for a sparkle in the eye, a special inner thrill at being on stage. Some dogs just simply seem to be born to it.

Needless to say, then, not every Malamute is cut out for the show ring. If showing is something that might interest you, think about that before you choose a puppy and work with a reputable breeder. He or she will guide you toward the show-quality puppies in a given litter, and, ideally, work with you to help foster the puppy's show talents. Keep in mind, however, that this does not mean the pet-quality Malamutes in that litter are any less valuable. They, too, have reaped the benefits of the careful breeding that produces fine show prospects and are destined to make, just as their name implies, the finest of pets. Their callings just happen to lie in directions other than that of the conformation show ring.

Obedience Trials

One of the callings that may be of interest to a Malamute owner is obedience competition. Be warned, however, that because of its independent spirit and strong-willed ideas about what it will and will not do, the Malamute's is not a face one commonly sees in the winner's circle at obedience trials. Yet there are dedicated owners who have set the earning of obedience titles as goals for their dogs, and they have succeeded.

At obedience trials, which are typically held in conjunction with conformation shows and are usually sanctioned by either the American Kennel Club or the United Kennel Club, dogs exhibit their ability to obey specific commands. The demands on the dogs grow increasingly challenging depending on the level of the titles for which they are competing.

Obedience offers all dogs an opportunity to shine regardless of their fitness as conformation show competitors, and it provides the ideal outlet for dogs and owners to work together as a team toward a common goal. While the canine component of the team usually understands that goal and is thrilled to participate, stories abound of Malamutes that have worked diligently for months, and then, when it's time for the real test, choose to exercise the legendary Malamute sense of humor and conveniently forget all that they have been taught. The main ingredient, then, for the owner who chooses to

Malamutes don't commonly become obedience champions, but they can enjoy the activity if both they and their owners approach it with a sense of humor.

Participating in a variety of activities with an Alaskan Malamute will only strengthen the legendary bond this dog shares with those it calls family.

For centuries, the Malamute's physique has been molded into one ideally suited to pulling weight.

compete with a Malamute in obedience is a sense of humor equal to that of the dog's.

Activities for Every Malamute

Organized events in which dogs can participate abound. This comes as good news for people who would like to be involved in such activities with

Weight pulling is a time honored Malamute activity that extends back to the days of Alaska's gold rush.

their dogs, but thought that conformation showing was the only option.

The weight pull: One such option open to Malamutes is weight pulling. While Siberian huskies and Alaskan huskies are considered the quintessential racing dogs, Malamutes occupy their own unique niche as kings of the weight pullers.

On its surface—and in the works of Jack London—weight pulling may appear somewhat cruel, but weight pulling is actually a very civilized activity (more so than it was during the rush for Yukon gold), and the dogs trained to participate, including Malamutes, relish the opportunity to make their owners proud. The International Weight Pull Association sponsors weight pulls in which dogs of various breeds and mixes of breeds compete in appropriate weight categories, pulling either sleds or wheeled carts for specified distances in prescribed time limits.

This activity obviously requires a commitment from the owner to the dog's training and conditioning, time spent that simultaneously fosters a unique and historical bond between the two. The dog is initially introduced to the special weight-training harness and the sensation of pulling very light weights. As the animal's strength and inclination develop, with the help of daily workouts and an athlete's diet, the weight is gradually increased. Once the load is too heavy for the dog, it will typically sit or stand still, the universal signal that it has finished for the day.

Attend an organized weight pull, and you will witness the beauty of a unique bond that can exist between a human being and a dog. Watch the dogs as they strive to please the people they call their own, and listen to those people as they encourage their dogs, speaking softly to them in a language that only they share. By the end of the day, you will understand just why the

Malamute has been known to bring tears to the eyes of full-grown men.

Agility: Agility events are often held in conjunction with more traditional conformation shows, and you are likely to find quite a large gathering of spectators congregating to witness these exciting events. Both agility training and the events themselves offer dog owners fun alternatives to more formal dog showing, and there is no better way to keep both dog and owner healthy, active, and young at heart.

When competing in this activity, the dog, with the coaching of its owner, makes its way through a canine obstacle course designed to showcase the dog's agility. Running, jumping, traversing, bobbing, and weaving, it attempts to complete the course quickly and with as few faults as possible, all to the enthusiastic cheers of the crowd. Needless to say, mastering agility skills requires training and conditioning, but the fun element is supreme. Win or lose, agility is a delightful event that, not surprisingly, is increasing in popularity each year.

Canine Good Citizen: Finally, when considering formal activities that you and your dog can pursue together, don't forget the American Kennel Club's Canine Good Citizen test. The CGC is a special title a dog can earn that proves to the world that this animal is the ideal canine companion.

To earn those coveted initials, the dog must pass several tests, which may require a bit of training ahead of time. The dog seeking this high acco-

Once he or she chooses to breed a litter of Malamute puppies, the ethical breeder makes a commitment to the well-being of those pups for the remainder of their lives.

lade for its good citizenship must exhibit its mastery of basic obedience commands; it must permit a stranger to pet, touch, and brush it; it must walk on a leash without pulling (fortunately for the Malamute, it need not do this at the heel); and it must show that it can ignore visual and sound distractions.

This is not a simple test for all dogs to pass, but those letters "CGC" after a dog's name are indeed something of which both dog and owner may be eternally proud. As an added bonus, once earned, the CGC opens an infinite number of doors to the dog, for the better citizen a dog is, the more welcome it will be wherever it may roam.

Useful Addresses and Literature

Organizations

The Alaskan Malamute Club of
America
Leslie Valiunas, Corresponding
Secretary
22W080 Temple Drive
Medinah, IL 60157

The Alaskan Malamute
Protection League, Inc.
Virginia Devaney
P.O. Box 170
Cedar Crest, NM 87008

The American Kennel Club
51 Madison Avenue
New York, NY 10010
Customer Service:
(919) 233-9767

The Canadian Kennel Club
89 Skyway Avenue, Suite 100
Etobicoke, Ontario, Canada
M9W 6R4
(416) 675-5511

Health Organizations

The Orthopedic Foundation for
Animals
2300 Nifong Boulevard
Columbia, MO 65201
(573) 442-0418

The AMCA Chondrodysplasia
Certification Committee
588 Lower Cleveland Rapids
Road
Roseburg, OR 97470

Periodicals

The Alaskan Malamute Club of
America Newsletter
200 Rhodes Road
Tolland, CT 06084

The American Kennel Club
Gazette
51 Madison Avenue
New York, NY 10010

Dog Fancy Magazine
P.O. Box 6050
Mission Viejo, CA 92690

Dog World Magazine
29 N. Wacker Drive
Chicago, IL 60606

Mushing Magazine
P.O. Box 149
Ester, AK 99725

Books

Baer, Ted, *Communicating with
Your Dog*, Barron's
Educational Series, Inc.,
Hauppauge, NY, 1989.
Campbell, William, *Behavior
Problems in Dogs*, American
Veterinary Publications, Inc.,
Goleta, CA, 1992.
Carlson, Delbert G., D.V.M., and
Griffin, James M., M.D., *Dog
Owner's Home Veterinary
Handbook*, Howell Book
House, New York, NY, 1992.

Christiansen, Bob, *Choosing a
Shelter Dog*, Canine Learning
Center Publishing Division,
Carlsbad, CA, 1995.
Dunbar, Ian, and Bohnenkamp,
Gwen, *Behaviour Booklets*
(various subjects), Center for
Applied Animal Behaviour,
Berkeley, CA, 1986.
Frye, Fredric, *First Aid for Your
Dog*, Barron's Educational
Series, Inc., Hauppauge, NY,
1987.
Kilcommons, Brian, and Wilson,
Sarah, *Good Owners, Great
Dogs*, Warner Books, 1992.
McDaniel, Jack and Colleen,
*Pooches & Small Fry: Parent-
ing Skills for Dogs and Kids*,
Doral Publishing, Inc.,
Wilsonville, OR, 1995.
Riddle, Maxwell, and Harris, Beth
J., *The New Complete Alaskan
Malamute*, Howell Book
House, New York, NY, 1990.
Siegal, Mordecai, *UC Davis
Book of Dogs*, HarperCollins
Publishers, New York, NY,
1995.
Wrede, Barbara, *Civilizing Your
Puppy*, Barron's Educational
Series, Inc., Hauppauge, NY,
1992.

Index